English for Business

English for Business

W. FERRIER MAVOR MA, FRSA

Pitman

PITMAN PUBLISHING LIMITED
39 Parker Street, London WC2B 5PB

Associated Companies
Copp Clark Ltd, Toronto
Fearon-Pitman Publishers Inc, Belmont, California
Pitman Publishing New Zealand Ltd, Wellington
Pitman Publishing Pty Ltd, Melbourne

© Pitman Publishing Ltd 1971

First published in Great Britain 1971
Reprinted 1973, 1974, 1976, 1978

All rights reserved. No part of this publication may be reproduced,
stored in a retrieval system, or transmitted, in any form or by any
means, electronic, mechanical, photocopying, recording and/or
otherwise without the prior written permission of the publishers.
This book may not be lent, resold, hired out or otherwise disposed of
by way of trade in any form of binding or cover other than that in
which it is published, without the prior consent of the publishers.

Reproduced and printed by photolithography and bound in
Great Britain at The Pitman Press, Bath

ISBN 0 273 00464 6

Preface

English for Business is both a textbook and a reference book with the following aims—to help students towards a more concise, lucid and correct expression of English, to provide model forms of business communications, to supply a wide range of exercises for training and practice, to stimulate interest in words and their function, and most important of all, to illustrate the force of simple and direct English.

I have presumed some knowledge of English grammar, thus allowing an immediate start with Sentence Construction. I have dealt with Minutes and Reports in simple form only, to provide an easily understandable introduction to these more complex aspects of Business English. In the middle chapters I have tried to emphasize and illustrate the importance of business letters.

English for Business is written for the young student at school and college studying secretarial and commercial subjects as a training for entry into business. It also aims to provide revision-practice for the older person seeking to break into the office field.

I should like to thank my former teaching colleagues who have helped so much with criticisms and suggestions—in particular, Mr. G. N. Forster, Mr. V. B. Reid, and Mrs. G. D. Hague.

F.M.

Contents

Preface   v

1. Sentence Construction   1
2. Direct and Indirect Speech   9
3. Punctuation   13
4. Spelling   18
5. Common Grammatical Errors   27
6. Accuracy of Expression   38
7. A Business-like Style   45
8. Planning a Business Letter   50
9. Different Types of Business Letter   59
10. The Art of Précis   115
11. Minutes and Reports   141
12. Comprehension Exercises   155
13. Abbreviations, and Foreign Words and Phrases   173
14. Test Papers   180

–1–

Sentence Construction

Your English should always be clear in its meaning, never loose or vague. It is essential therefore to have a sound knowledge of sentence construction, for how can we write clearly unless we know how to build meaningful sentences?

The basis of all English composition is the sentence. A sentence has two parts, a subject with which it deals, and a predicate, the part that says something about the subject.

Simple Sentences

Here are some examples—

Subject	*Predicate*
Your order of 9th May	has already been dispatched.
Mr. Andrews of our Export Branch	will call on you next Monday.
The name of the firm	is the Northern Timber Co., Ltd.
The outlook for the next quarter	is not very encouraging.
Taking out the machinery	has been difficult.

The predicate necessarily contains a verb, "has been dispatched," "will call," "is," "has been." Without a verb a sentence does not make complete sense and we call it a phrase.

The five examples given above have only one subject and only one verb, and are therefore known as simple sentences.

Complex Sentences

Look at this sentence—

> We shall be glad to know the day on which you can call at this office to complete the transaction.

This sentence has two different subjects, "we" and "you," and two verbs—"shall be glad to know" and "can call"—and is therefore a complex sentence. In a complex sentence we have a principal clause—"We shall be glad to know the day" and a subordinate clause or clauses—"on which you can call at this office to complete the transaction."

Take another example. Here are four simple sentences—

> My friend Dawson called at my house last night.
> This made me glad.
> He wanted to discuss our final plans.
> We are going to Paris in a week's time.

They can be combined in one complex sentence—

> I was glad when my friend Dawson called at my house last night to discuss our final plans for our visit to Paris next week.

EXERCISE I

1. Construct a single complex sentence from each of the following—

   (*a*) This morning I received a letter from the travel agents. They told me that we should have to change our route. There had been a railway accident at Rouen.

   (*b*) We have been developing sports and recreation grounds. This has been done over the past two years. The grounds are on the boundary of Thorncliffe. They will soon be one of the finest works sports grounds in the country. Up to the present we have been allowed to erect only temporary buildings. They are actually converted army huts. We hope in due course to replace them with permanent buildings.

EXERCISE II

1. Combine the following in two complex sentences—

   (a) A crate of ornaments was delivered this morning by your van. It appears to be the fulfilment of our order sent last week. Not all the items on our list have been sent. Three of the Worcester figures were broken. We are returning these. We are also sending a list of those not sent. We shall be glad to have the latter and replacement of the breakages forwarded as soon as possible.

   (b) My colleagues and I are thinking of the future role of your company. This role is that of an investment trust. It is our duty to earn dividends for our stockholders; but the function of the trust should extend beyond that of mere collectors of dividends. We feel this strongly. We should ensure that the funds at our disposal are used to the best advantage. This should be in the interests of industry in this country and in development overseas under private enterprise. In the latter sphere this company has a contribution to make.

Variety in Construction

It is the varied use of simple and complex sentences in a letter or other composition which preserves it from monotony. It is possible to link two or more simple sentences by conjunctions or connecting words, e.g. *and*, *but*. Such sentences are called compound sentences because they consist of more than one principal clause. Look at the following sentences—

   (a) The dealer went to the depot and collected his issue of stores.

This sentence has two principal clauses.

(b) He hoped to get his supplies cheaply, but found that there was only a limited quantity available and as a result had to pay higher prices.

This sentence has three principal clauses.

EXERCISE III

1. Combine the following simple sentences into compound sentences by the use of conjunctions—

    (a) The makers are busy. They cannot meet our demands.
    (b) Our agent was unable to call this week. He will make an effort to see you on Monday.
    (c) We prefer the No. 2 quality. We are willing, in the circumstances, to accept the next best.

Below are further examples of variety in composition. Look at this sentence—

> Arthur lives in a house with a southern aspect, set on the side of a hill, and from his front windows he has a view of the sea.

Now note the variations possible—

(a) Living in a house set on the southern side of a hill, Arthur can see the sea from his windows.
(b) By looking out of his front windows, Arthur can see the sea, since his house is built on the side of a hill and faces south.
(c) From the front windows of Arthur's house, which is built on the hillside facing south, he has the sea in view.

EXERCISE IV

1. Take the following sentences and vary the construction so as to give the facts in different forms—

    (a) The materials we use in our productions are the best obtainable. Our workmen are skilled and highly trained.

As a result we have secured a leading position as producers of up-to-date machines.

(b) Satisfied that he had done his best in John's interest, his father felt that the final issue must depend on his son's good sense and willingness to co-operate.

Complex Sentences

The complex sentence gives the greatest variety of style. See how this simple sentence may be developed—

Trade shows signs of improvement.

(a) Trade *now* shows signs of improvement *in this area*.

"Now" is an *adverb* marking the time; "in this area" is an *adverbial phrase* which marks the place of improvement.

(b) *Since the year turned* trade shows signs of improvement in the areas *in which we have opened new branches*.

"Since the year turned" is a clause substituted for the adverb "now" and is called an *Adverbial Clause of Time*. "In which we have opened new branches" is a clause marking the "areas" as would an adjective and is called an *Adjectival Clause*.

EXERCISE V

1. Form complex sentences with adverbial clauses—

   (a) We shall be glad to supply this information. We have consulted Head Office.
   (b) Will you be good enough to explain? You arrived at this conclusion.
   (c) This can be easily remedied. You have sent us the broken article.
   (d) Put the box somewhere in the store-room. We can find it.
   (e) There will be no opportunity to arrange a meeting. They are in the city next week.

2. Form complex sentences with adjectival clauses—

   (a) Henry Jones succeeded to the business. His father had founded it.

   (b) The parcel arrived today. We ordered it over a week ago.

   (c) The men receive a bonus. They have earned it.

   (d) I am sending you the copy of the statement. You asked for it.

   (e) Close attention to details is the key. It ensures accuracy.

Long and Short Sentences

Long sentences and short sentences have their appropriate uses. A succession of short sentences may be used to emphasize quick action or tension.

For example—

> Jones saw his opportunity. The Chairman had finished speaking. The men seemed undecided. Jones pushed back his chair and got to his feet. He looked down at the factory floor. All the men waited for him to speak.

The same sequence of events may also be described, less dramatically, in this way—

> As the Chairman finished speaking to the men, Jones, in their indecision, saw his opportunity. He pushed back his chair and, getting to his feet, looked down at the factory floor where the men stood waiting for him to speak.

Now look at these two passages.

(a) When first in the dim light of early morning I saw the shores of Cuba rise and define themselves from dark-blue horizons, I felt as if I sailed with Long John Silver and first gazed on Treasure Island. Here was a place where real things were going on. Here was a scene of vital action. Here was a place where anything might happen. Here was a place where something would certainly happen. Here I might leave my bones. These musings were dispersed by the advance of breakfast, and lost in the hurry of disembarkation.

Extract from *My Early Life* (Churchill)

Did you note the stirring effect of the five short sentences each beginning with "Here."?

(b) It may be remarked in the course of this little conversation (which took place as the coach rolled along lazily by the river-side) that, though Miss Rebecca Sharp has twice had occasion to thank Heaven, it has been, in the first place, for ridding her of some person whom she hated, and, secondly, for enabling her to bring her enemies to some sort of perplexity or confusion, neither of which is a very amiable motive for religious gratitude, or such as would be put forward by persons of a kind and placable disposition.

Extract from *Vanity Fair* (Thackeray)

Did you note the measured build-up of this single complex sentence?

Try to avoid monotony in your writing. Remember that short and long sentences may be intermingled.

Short sentences are used—

(a) to express rapidity of event, motion or dramatic or tense situations
(b) to drive home points or to sum up an argument
(c) in definitions

Longer sentences are used—

(a) in descriptive passages
(b) to develop a reasoned argument
(c) to build up background
(d) to give weight and dignity to the writing

EXERCISE VI

1. Combine this series of short sentences into complex sentences—

    (*a*) It was no time to be sorry. We did what had to be done. The ammunition situation was bad. The ammunition had been hidden for a long time. It might be damp. Some of it was not reliable.

    (*b*) Susan is usually a good tennis player. This week her game has been very ragged. She has played a lot of good strokes. Her base-line returns too often break down. It seems that she is over-played. This alone must have an adverse effect.

2. Describe (*a*) in short sentences, (*b*) in complex sentences, the scene in an upstairs office when a fire alarm is sounded in the building.

–2–

Direct and Indirect Speech

When a writer reports the actual words spoken by a person, he is using direct speech. Here is an example—

Mr. Jones then said, "Mr. Chairman, I regret that I must oppose the motion."

This may be turned into indirect speech by writing—

Mr. Jones said that he regretted he must oppose the motion.

Certain changes are necessary when converting direct speech into indirect speech. They are as follows—

1. The conjunction *that* is inserted before the reported words, except in a question.
2. Tense sequence must be followed. For example—
   (*a*) If the reporting verb is in the past tense, the verbs that follow must also be in the past tense.
   (*b*) If the reporting verb is in the present or future tense, the verbs that follow may be in any tense.
3. First and second personal pronouns become third person, i.e. *I* and *you* become *he*.
4. The adjective *this* becomes *that*, and *these* becomes *those*.
5. Adverbs of time and place alter. For example—
   now becomes *then*; *today* becomes *that day*; *tomorrow* becomes *the next day*; *yesterday* becomes the *day before*

Watch the following points—

1. When converting from indirect to direct speech, punctuation calls for particular attention. It is important not to forget that inverted commas enclose the actual spoken word. Also, the reporting verb e.g. *said, replied,* etc., should be followed by a comma or colon.

    A quotation made within the words spoken should be enclosed in a single set of inverted commas. For example—

    Both men replied, "We are sure we heard Mr. Brown say 'I agree to the plan put forward.' "

2. When reporting questions, you should use a verb indicating that a question has been asked. For example—

    He said, "May I have your views on the proposal?"

    In reported speech this becomes—

    He asked if he might have his views on the proposal.

3. When possible, vary the reporting verbs. Here are some—*said, remarked, continued, suggested, replied, told, explained, observed,* etc. This variation helps to avoid monotony.

EXERCISE I

1. Convert the following from direct to indirect speech—

    (*a*) The manager said, "I am not going to keep you long, but I want you to understand that this company will not be a party to any underhand dealing such as has been proposed."

    (*b*) Our competitors say, "You have enjoyed a monopoly of this business for a good many years; we now intend to secure a footing in this market."

    (*c*) "Do you suppose," he went on, "that I can support you in your undertaking?"

    (*d*) "Can you tell me," she asked, "where I can find the office-manager?"

(e) "If you will tell me," I said, "which points you wish included in the report, then I shall see what can be done about them."

2. The following passages are reported speech; re-write them, giving the words actually spoken.

(a) Introducing the guest, the chairman said they were delighted to welcome him. He was not only a man well-known in public life, but he had had long experience in business and could be relied upon to give them much good advice.

(b) I told him I should always be interested in his progress after he left us and that I should look forward to his visits whenever he returned to London.

(c) The present position, said the director, referring to the tabled report, was the result of inefficiency in the supply section. He urged that someone be appointed to examine the causes of such ineptitude.

(d) It seemed to him, the customer said, that the dealer was more concerned with selling a particular line of goods which would yield him a good profit than with supplying the article which he himself had been looking for.

(e) The speaker informed the meeting that he had come there at some inconvenience, and, since he had had very short notice, he might not be able to deal with the matter on which he had been consulted as fully as they might wish. He would endeavour however to clear up the main points and to answer any questions that they might put to him.

EXERCISE II

1. Turn this speech into reported form, beginning with the words —The Chairman thought . . .

"It is, I think, fitting that I should close these remarks with a word of appreciation of the continuing support given me by my predecessor in office, the present chairman of the board; and also that I should add a comment called forth by the resignation of Mr. Arthur Cross, formerly president and latterly chairman of the board.

The retirement of Mr. Cross from office in the corporation removes a notable figure in its history, to whom in no small measure the credit is due for the sound financial position which the corporation has attained, and whose own character and qualities have contributed greatly to the creation of the *esprit de corps* and high morale which pervade the organisation from top to bottom."

2. Convert this passage into direct speech, beginning: "The last meeting," said the chairman, "was too prolonged, and I hope . . .

The chairman said that the previous meeting had been too prolonged and expressed the wish that there should not be a repetition of the delaying tactics which certain members had used. He was determined to keep strictly to the agenda. Several members were annoyed. Mr. Brown expressed his regret that the chairman's comment had been so brusque. It was in some ways an unnecessary slight on the members' characters. The chairman interrupted to say that such a slight had not been intended.

Punctuation

What is punctuation and why do we use it? It is, quite simply, the use of stops or breaks to indicate pauses in the flow of language so that meaning may be clearly defined. There are, of course, secondary uses of these stops—to indicate quotations; to show that a remark is to be taken as a question or as an explanation; to separate items on a list.

The chief marks of punctuation are as follows—

FULL STOP. This is used—

(*a*) to denote the end of a sentence

(*b*) after initials or abbreviations, e.g. W. F. Smith; Messrs.; Col. Brown; cum div.; ad val.

(*c*) in numerical indications of time, to separate hours and minutes, e.g. 10.30 hrs

(*d*) to signify that words have been omitted; normally there are three dots if the omission is in the middle of a sentence, four when the omission occurs after a completed sentence.

Note that a full stop is not necessary—

(*a*) after such symbols as 1st, 2nd, 4th

(*b*) after words or figures used in tabular work (except decimal points)

(*c*) when an abbreviation ends in the same letter as the original words, e.g. yd for yard

(*d*) at the end of a heading

COMMA. This indicates the shortest marked pause in a sentence. One of its main uses is to separate words in a list—

> Dealing with the profit and loss account, the chairman called attention to the fact that the expense items under wages, salaries, repairs, and taxes all showed a substantial increase.

Some grammarians make it a rule not to use the comma before "and" in a list. In common with Fowler, I believe that the comma used before "and" can often avoid ambiguity.

For example, "black, white, and green" refers to three objects each of a single different colour. "Black, white and green, and red", on the other hand, refers to three objects one of which is in two colours, white and green.

SEMI-COLON. This has almost the strength of the full stop, and is used when two statements are closely connected in thought but are not linked grammatically, for example—

> The committee held the view that the matter should receive further consideration; they recommended that the secretary should make more detailed inquiries and report at the next meeting.

COLON. This is not often used in continuous composition. Normally it introduces a series or an enumeration—

> The items discussed were: (*a*) time and place of the next meeting, (*b*) remuneration of agents, (*c*) allotment of areas to each representative.

INVERTED COMMAS. These are used to enclose the actual words spoken—

> Speaking with obvious sincerity he said, "I shall never forget your kindness."

They are also used in quotations—

> "a rose by any other name would smell as sweet" (Shakespeare)

Another use of the inverted comma is when mentioning the title of a book, play or publication.

For example—

He read it in "The Times."

APOSTROPHE. This indicates the possessive case, as in "Jane's handbag," or the omission of a letter or letters—"There's no point in hurrying; we can't get home in time now."

It also signifies the plural of abbreviations, letters, and figures—"a number of M.P.'s"; "there are five 5's in twenty-five and two m's in accommodation."

EXCLAMATION MARK. As the name implies this is used after exclamatory words, phrases or sentences, indicating surprise, shock or impatience—

"Alas!"; "Heavens! Look what you've done!"; "A fine friend you are!"

QUESTION MARK or QUERY. This should follow every question if a separate answer is required to each question, e.g. "Did you see the man? Where did he go?" (The inverted commas are always placed after the question mark)

DASH. This marks a parenthesis, e.g.—

A week later—at the end of May—he handed in his resignation.

It is sometimes used to introduce an interpolation, as in—

He asked me—despite the fact that I was a complete stranger to him—to support his nomination.

It is also used to sum up or gather a scattered subject, e.g.

Bells, whistles, sirens, hooters—all welcomed the yacht as she entered the river.

HYPHEN. This joins two or more words which are looked on as one, e.g. "rag-and-bone man." Often this joining becomes permanent, as in "to-day" and "to-morrow," now written as one, "today" and "tomorrow."

The most common use of the hyphen is to divide into syllables a word broken up because of lack of space; the hyphen should be introduced early in the word, e.g. "dis-enchanted," not "disenchant-ed," or in the middle, e.g. "inter-woven." You should always avoid cutting off the suffix *-ed*. If in any doubt about where to put the hyphen, always take the Concise Oxford English Dictionary as your guide.

Points to note

1. Only the more common marks of punctuation have been covered in this chapter.

2. In business today the trend is towards as little punctuation as possible. You should remember that the use of too many stops tends to break the flow of the written word (*see* pages 55–56 for an account of the fully-blocked open-punctuated form of letter). Study this example—

   When you were in London in June, we did agree, I think, that 1st January would be a suitable delivery date and, whilst I can scarcely argue, in view of the quantity of unsaleable stock of the current edition, that a month or two will make very much difference, nevertheless, I do feel that the sooner we publish the better.

   Now look at it written with the minimum of punctuation—

   When you were in London in June we did agree, I think, that 1st January would be a suitable delivery date and whilst I can scarcely argue, in view of the quantity of unsaleable stock of the current edition, that a month or two will make very much difference, nevertheless I do feel that the sooner we publish the better.

3. A change in punctuation may alter meaning considerably, e.g.

   (*a*) I lost my wallet however; it was found in John's room.

   (*b*) I lost my wallet; however it was found in John's room.

EXERCISES

Punctuate the following—

1. The point surely is this does the Committee intend to consider an increase in the secretarys salary if so in what amount meantime until this question has been discussed in committee nothing can be done it would be of benefit perhaps to call a meeting as soon as possible which day next week would be convenient
2. Can you tell me he asked why we havent seen you for weeks
3. These are the things you will have to provide for the expedition food water warm clothing tents cooking stoves blankets and make sure theyre at the quay in good time
4. Enterprise energy enthusiasm these are basic requirements for success in any undertaking
5. You have been told that the essentials of a business letter are lucidity conciseness and courtesy can you suggest any other important point to be borne in mind
6. Halt who goes there
7. The notice read gone to lunch back at 2.30
8. Further to yesterdays telephone call I enclose a note of the fee payable namely £4.50
9. He had a sullen almost oxeyed look about him
10. The typist finds Mr Browns reports very hard to decipher his as and us are so much alike

–4–

Spelling

Why is the spelling of English so awkward and difficult? There are possibly two reasons. The English language has many more sounds in it than letters. Because of this some of its letters do a double task, representing more than one sound. In the words *pate* and *pat*, for instance, the letter *a* carries two different sounds; in *poke* and *pot* the letter *o* differs very much in sound.

Consonants as well as vowels carry varying sounds, e.g. *cake* and *cinema* where the *c* is first hard, then soft in sound; note also the difference in the *g* sounds in *give* and *gem*.

Moreover, English is a mongrel language, having benefited from the many invaders of different nationalities who have, in time past, staked claim on British soil. The Vikings, Saxons, Romans and Normans have all contributed their share to the English language. This accounts for many difficulties in pronunciation and spelling.

Dough, *cough* and *enough*, for instance, are three words that are Anglo-Saxon in origin, which we pronounce quite differently, though each is spelt -*ough*. *Mile* and *Century* and the names of the months in the year we owe to the Romans, whereas *bottle*, *boat* and *flower* are all French in origin.

This diversity in the English language makes it difficult to lay down hard and fast rules. Nevertheless, there are some ways in which you can overcome your spelling difficulties.

You can—
(a) Learn the 200 most commonly misspelt words listed at the end of this chapter. (They constitute a quarter of all spelling mistakes.)
(b) Learn the more common prefixes and suffixes.
(c) Make yourself familiar with some of the more simple rules.
(d) Consult a dictionary when in doubt.

Correct spelling is an essential requirement for accurate communication. Words are the tools you use to express your ideas. Like all tools they are valuable only when correctly used. It is not enough to add a long list of correctly-spelled words to your vocabulary. They need exercise! The more writing you do the better.

Prefixes

Dis-, Un- and Mis-

Study these words—disappoint, unclean, mistake. In each case a prefix, *dis-*, *un-*, *mis-* has been added to its word, *appoint, clean, take*, without any change being made to the word.

If the word begins with the same letter as the last letter of the prefix, then there will be a double consonant. For example—

dissatisfied	ennoble	innumerable
dissertation	illegible	misshapen
dissipate	illicit	misspell
dissolve	immodest	unnatural

For- and Fore-

The prefixes *for-* and *fore-* need careful attention. *For-* often implies a prohibition or abstention, *fore-* means "before." In this group therefore be guided by the meaning.

forbade	forebode
forborne	forehead
forgiveness	forerunner
forsake	forestall
forswear	foretell

Remember! *Forgo* means "to go without" and *forego* means "to go before."

Con-, Com-, Col- and Cor-

The Latin prefix *cum*, meaning *with*, is at the root of these prefixes, though it has suffered a slight change in each instance. In each case the third letter of the prefix agrees with the first consonant of the root word. For example—

connive	commit	collect	correct
connect	commune	collusion	corrode
connote	commodious	collapse	correspond
connoisseur	commend	collaborate	correlate

Pre-, Pro- and Per-

These prefixes also call for careful pronunciation. Here are some examples of each which you should learn.

prescribe and proscribe; precede and proceed;
prefer and proffer; persecute and prosecute;

Terminations and Suffixes

-able and -ible

The final "e" is usually dropped before *-able* and *-ible*.

The following are examples.

conceivable	collapsible
dissolvable	forcible
excitable	producible
movable	reducible

There are always exceptions to the rule, and with words ending in *-able* and *-ible*, the exceptions are quite often in those words ending in "g" or "c," where the "e" is retained to give the soft sound. For instance—

changeable	noticeable
manageable	peaceable
marriageable	serviceable

Further exceptions are—*rateable, saleable*.

SPELLING

-ary, -ery, -ory and -ry

It is easy to get confused over the spelling of words with these endings. The only thing to do is learn them. Here are some common examples.

-ary	*-ery*	*-ory*	*-ry*
boundary	cemetery	advisory	foundry
secretary	imagery	desultory	idolatry
sedentary	monastery	dormitory	sentry

Especially confusing are *stationery* the noun meaning "paper", etc, and *stationary* the adjective meaning "fixed" or "motionless."

-ar, -er, -or, -ur and -re

Words with these endings are also easy to confuse. Again, the only solution to the problem is to learn the words. A particularly topical mistake is the spelling of "metre" and "meter." The fully decimal-conscious secretary should never make the mistake of spelling "metre" the measurement as "meter" the measurer.

-ar-	*-er*	*-or*	*-ur & -re*
beggar	barometer	auditor	murmur
grammar	heifer	author	sulphur
muscular	traveller	councillor	theatre
singular	labourer	doctor	spectre

-ceed, -cede and -ede

Again, observation of each word is the best way of mastering its spelling. Learn the words in the table below.

-ceed	*-cede*	*-ede*
exceed	accede	impede
proceed	concede	recede
succeed	intercede	supersede

-our and -or

Do not use the American *-or* in words like—honour, labour, favour.

N.B. clamour, clamorous
honour, honourable, honorary, honorarium
humour, humorous
vigour, vigorous

-fer and -cur

When the syllable *-fer* is to stressed and is followed by a vowel, the *r* must be doubled. For example—

(*a*) confer, conference, conferred, conferring.
defer, deference, deferred, deferring.
prefer, preference, preferred, preferring.
refer, reference, referee, referred, referring.

The same applies to words ending in *-cur*

For example—

(*b*) concur, concurring, concurred, concurrence.
demur, demurring, demurred, demurrage.
occur, occurring, occurred, occurrence.
recur, recurring, recurred, recurrence, recurrent.

If the *r* is not doubled before a following vowel, the *u* will sound like the *u* in *secured*.

The Double L

Mistakes often occur when *-ed* and *-ing* are added to verbs ending in *l*.

The rule is—

Double the *l* if it is preceded by a single vowel, as in—

compel, compelling; control, controlled.

But, if it is preceded by a pair of vowels, the *l* is not doubled, as in—

wail, wailing; hail, hailed.

Adverbs

An adverb formed from an adjective ending in *l* has this *l* doubled, e.g.

special, specially; general, generally.

An adverb formed from an adjective already ending in double *l* does not need a third *l*, e.g. *dully, fully*.

An adverb formed from an adjective ending in *-ic* adds, for its ending, *-ically*, e.g. *basically, specifically, heroically*.

But note the exception, *publicly*.

Watch the spelling of *wholly, truly* and *duly* from the adjectives *whole, true* and *due*.

Nouns and Verbs

There are some pairs of words in which the verb is spelt with an *s* and the noun with a *c;* you must learn not to confuse these.

The verbs are—*license, practise, advise, devise, prophesy*.
The nouns are—*licence, practice, advice, device, prophecy*.

"i" before "e" except after "c".

This is a good rule, but you must remember that it applies only when the "ie" and "ei" rhyme with "key."
Here are some examples—

achieve	liege	ceiling
believe	piece	conceive
brief	shriek	deceive
chief	siege	perceive
grieve	thief	receipt

Note that in the third column the order is "e" before "i" because they follow the "c."

When "ie" and "ei" have any other sound than that of "key," the order is "ei" as in—

deign	freight	inveigle	rein
eider	heifer	leisure	skein
eight	heighten	neigh	sleigh
feint	heir	obeisance	sleight

Foreign Plurals

Some words always keep their foreign plurals. For example—

Singular	*Plural*
agendum	agenda
bureau	bureaux
crisis	crises
criterion	criteria
datum	data
erratum	errata
hypothesis	hypotheses
memorandum	memoranda
minimum	minima
oasis	oases
phenomenon	phenomena
thesis	theses
tableau	tableaux

Some words have an English plural as well as a foreign plural form, e.g. *formulas* and *formulae; appendixes* and *appendices*.

If in doubt prefer an English plural to an incorrect foreign plural.

200 MOST COMMONLY MISSPELT WORDS

absence	colleagues	familiar	medicine	proprietary
accidentally	coming	February	Mediterranean	psychology
accommodate	committee	financial	miniature	quiet
achieved	comparative	foreign	minutes	really
acknowledge	competent	forty	mischievous	received
acquainted	completely	friend	murmur	recognize
addresses	conscientious	fulfilled	necessary	recommended
aerial	conscious	gauge	negotiate	referred
aggravate	consistent	genius	niece	relieved
aggregate	convenience	government	noticeable	repetition
agreeable	courteous	grammar	occasional	restaurant
all right	courtesy	grievance	occasionally	rhythm
amateur	criticism	guard	occurred	scarcely

SPELLING

among	deceive	guardian	occurrence	secretaries
analysis	decision	handkerchief	omitted	seize
Antarctic	definite	height	omission	sentence
anxiety	desirable	heroes	opinion	separate
apparent	desperate	honorary	originally	severely
appearance	disappeared	humorous	parallel	shining
appropriate	disappointed	hungry	parliament	similar
Arctic	disastrous	hurriedly	pastime	sincerely
argument	discipline	hypocrisy	permanent	statutory
arrangement	dissatisfied	imagination	permissible	successful
ascend	efficiency	immediately	perseverance	supersede
athletic	eighth	immigrate	personnel	suppression
automation	eliminated	incidentally	physical	surprising
awful	embarrassed	independent	planning	synonym
bachelor	emphasize	indispensable	pleasant	tendency
beginning	enthusiasm	influential	possesses	tragedy
believed	equipped	intelligence	preceding	transferred
benefited	especially	irresistible	preference	twelfth
beneficial	essential	knowledge	prejudice	unconscious
breathe	exaggerated	liaison	preliminary	undoubtedly
budgeted	excellent	literature	prestige	unnecessary
business	exercise	livelihood	privilege	until
ceiling	exhausted	lose	procedure	usually
certain	existence	losing	proceeds	valuable
choice	expenses	lying	professional	view
clothes	experience	maintenance	professor	Wednesday
college	extremely	marriage	pronunciation	woollen

EXERCISE I

1. Compose sentences to show the meaning of the following words—

    asterisk, auxiliary, collusion, connote, deign, ennoble, feint, foreboding, forego, inveigle, proffer, proscribe.

2. Form the negatives of the following words by adding prefixes—

    allow, favour, important, known, legal, lovely, loyal, noble, regular, reverence, trust, trustworthy.

EXERCISE II

1. Use the following words in sentences to show what they mean—

    abridgment, contagious, contention, discrepancy, fallacious, honorarium, intercede, licence, lucid, perceptible, privilege, prohibitive.

2. From these endings, *-ar*, *-er*, *-or*, *-ur*, *-re* complete the following words and in each case give the meaning—

aggress . .	counsell . .	lem . .
aug . .	hydromet. .	massac . .
cens . .	inc . .	somb . .
conjur . .	jur . .	tuss . .

3. Explain the meaning of—

    device, devise, licence, license

EXERCISE III

1. Introduce the following words into sentences—

    commission, condescend, indefinite, omission, precedence, recompense, temporarily.

2. Explain the meanings of—

    allergic, intrinsic, philanthropic, psychic, soporific.

3. Explain the following phrases and then use each of them correctly in a sentence—

established fact	poetic licence
incidental expenses	press release
interested party	secondary meaning
mass production	special edition
passive resistance	standard performance

4. Give the plural of the following—

    analysis, axis, focus, index, medium, radius, species, stamen, stratum, terminus.

–5–

Common Grammatical Errors

It may help to improve your written English if you know some of the errors into which it is all too easy to fall. You can then put yourself on guard against them. This chapter lists the more common grammatical errors in the hope that you will do just that.

Incorrect Agreement

1. When a verb is used after a pronoun it must agree with the word for which the pronoun stands.

"It is you who *is* to blame" is wrong. The word "who" stands for "you" and must be followed by the same verb as "you." Therefore we must say—"It is you who *are* to blame."

2. The Indefinite Pronoun *one* is used when making general statements, not applicable to anyone in particular. For example—

One must not brood over *one's* misfortunes.

The word *his* cannot refer to *one*. The sentence "*One* must sweep before *his* own door" is wrong, and must be "*One* must sweep before *one's* own door."

3. Collective Nouns take their verb in the singular. This is sometimes lost sight of when the subject is separated from the verb by several words or phrases. For example—

The bundle of books, magazines and papers *were* lying on the table.

Here the plural verb *were* is wrong, for the subject *bundle* is singular; therefore the verb must be in the singular, *was*.

> The bundle of books, magazines and papers *was* lying on the table.

N.B. A Collective Noun, in some instances, may take a plural verb. This occurs when the stress is on the individual items making up the collective noun rather than on the collective noun itself.

For example—

> The committee *was* unanimous when it came to voting.

But—

> The committee of directors *were* unanimous in the decision to vote.

4. The Relative Pronoun must agree with its antecedent in number and person. It takes its case from its own clause. Study these examples—

> (*a*) She is one of the most competent typists who *has* ever worked in the department.

The relative pronoun *who* has as its antecedent *typists* and therefore, being plural, must take a plural verb, *have*.

> (*b*) That is the man *who* Mr. Jones saw yesterday.

Here, *who* is wrong and must be *whom* as it is the object, in its own clause, of the verb *saw*.

> (*c*) That is the girl *who* I know was successful.

Here, *who* is correct as it is the subject of the verb *was*.

5. A noun or pronoun which is governed by a preposition is in the objective case. Care must be taken when two pronouns occur after a preposition.

> It will be impossible for you and *I*

This is wrong and ought to be—

> It will be impossible for you and *me*

The word *me* is in the objective case after *for*.

imilarly, "between *him* and *I*" is incorrect. This ought to be "between *him* and *me*."

6. *Either* is used to indicate one of two alternatives; otherwise *any* must be used.

> I do not approve of either of the suggestions.

Here, there are only two suggestions.

> I do not approve of *any* of the suggestions.

This means there are more than two suggestions.

N.B. The word *either* is singular and must take a singular verb.

> *Either* Mr. Brown or Mr. Jones *is* to be asked.

Similarly, *neither* is used of two things or persons and takes its verb in the singular.

> *Neither* of the girls intends coming.

This means that there are only two girls.
If more than two are meant, then *none* must be used, but note that *none* may take a singular or plural verb, according to sense. When it means *not any* it may be followed by a plural verb.

> *None* of the members *are* prepared to accept the decision.

But when it means *not a single one* it takes a singular verb.

> *None* of the class *is* prepared to come next Wednesday.

Either . . . . . . or: Neither . . . . . . nor. When two singular subjects are so connected, a singular verb is used.

> *Neither* Miss Smith *nor* Miss Black *was* present.

Comparison of Adjectives

An adjective has three degrees. The simple adjective is said to be positive—*sweet*; the adjective used to compare two objects is comparative—*sweeter*; and the adjective used to compare three or more objects is superlative—*sweetest*. It is important to use the correct degree. There are some common mistakes which it is easy to make.

"Which is your weakest eye?" ought to be "Which is your *weaker* eye?" because only two eyes are being compared.

"My book is the best of the two" ought to be "My book is the *better* of the two" because better is the comparative degree.

Faulty Ellipsis

It sometimes makes for a smoother style to shorten an expression by leaving out a word—instead of "It was revealed *to* and restored *to* him by an accident," we can say "It was revealed and restored to him by an accident."

This method of omitting words is called ellipsis. If by omitting a word we make the sentence incomplete or grammatically wrong, then the omission is called faulty ellipsis. For example—

Ships go and return from all parts of the world.

Here we say *return from*, but we should also say *go to*. The sentence then reads—

Ships go to and return from all parts of the world.

What is wrong with this sentence?

I always have and always will look upon him as a friend.

Here *will look* is correct, but *looked* is required after *have*. The sentence then becomes—

I always have looked and always will look upon him as a friend.

Mistakes in Verb Usage

1. The correct *Sequence of Tenses* must be observed. In narrative the tense of a verb ought not be changed unnecessarily.

    N.B. If the principal verb of a sentence is in the past tense, the subordinate verbs must also be in the past tense; but a principal verb in the present tense may be followed by any tense. Here are some examples of incorrect and correct sequence of tenses—
    - (*a*) He said that he *will* take the letters to post. (incorrect)
      He said that he *would* take the letters to post. (correct)
    - (*b*) I shall be happy if you *would* come. (incorrect)
      I shall be happy if you *will* come. (correct)
    - (*c*) I thought I *shall* be unable to go. (incorrect)
      I *think* I shall be unable to go. (correct)

If you remember to be consistent in your choice of tenses, you won't go far wrong.

COMMON GRAMMATICAL ERRORS

2. *The Split Infinitive* (the insertion of a word between *to* and the verb) should be avoided. Its use is both cumbersome and untidy. Therefore, instead of writing "to thoroughly clean," or "to seriously consider," write "to clean thoroughly" and "to consider seriously."

3. *The Perfect Infinitive* needs attention. What is wrong with the following sentence?

He expected *to have seen* Mr. Brown yesterday.

The 'expecting' and the 'seeing' were to take place on the same day. It is therefore unnecessary to use *to have seen*. The sentence ought to read—

He expected *to see* Mr. Brown yesterday.

Here is another example—

I hoped *to have gone* with you today.

This could be simplified as follows—

I hoped *to go* with you today.

4. The verb *to be* takes the same case before and after.

N.B. The *subject* of a sentence is in the *nominative* case.
The *object* of a sentence is in the *objective* case.

When the verb *to be* or any part of it is used to connect two nouns or pronouns, these words must be in the same case.

"It is me" ought to be "It is I."

"It" is the subject (nominative case) and "I" (nominative case) must follow *is*.

"Whom do you think he is?" ought to be "Who do you think he is?"

Here the meaning conveyed is "He is who?" "He" is nominative and "who" must also be nominative because it follows *is*.

"Who do you believe him to be?" ought to be "Whom do you believe him to be?"

The meaning in fact is "You believe him to be whom?" "Him" is objective case and "whom" therefore must also be objective after the verb *to be*.

Errors of Syntax

1. Misplaced Pairs of Conjunctions

This often happens. The most common pairs of conjunctions are—

not only . . . but also; either . . . or; both . . . and.

Care should be taken about their positioning. For example—

He has *not only* shown himself to be discourteous *but also* careless in his attitude to work.

Here *not only* is out of position and ought to come immediately before "discourteous."

The flight is *either* scheduled for 1300 *or* 1400 hours.

The word *either* is in the wrong place here. The sentence should read—

The flight is scheduled for *either* 1300 *or* 1400 hours.

N.B. The second conjunction must be followed by the same part of speech as the first. Check this from the examples given above.

2. The Misuse of "as" and "like"

As is a conjunction but *like* is a comparative and must not be used as a conjunction. Study these examples—

I wish I could sing *like* you do.

Here the use of *like* as a conjunction is wrong. The sentence should read—

I wish I could sing *as* you do.

The word *like* is used correctly in this sentence.

She is *like* her mother.

3. The Placing of "only"

This word *only* is so very often misplaced. If you remember that it must be close to the word it modifies or explains it will help. For example—

I *only* saw him last week.

Only saw suggests that you did not speak to him or acknowledge him. The word *only* should really explain or add to the meaning of *last week*, and the sentence ought to be—

I saw him *only* last week.

4. "Owing to" and "due to"

These look easy, but they are, in fact, frequently misused. Perhaps they are difficult to differentiate. Try, then, to remember this—

Owing to relates to a verb, for example—

> She failed her examinations *owing to* her lack of interest.

Due to relates to a noun—

> John's failure was *due to* his lack of interest.

5. The End Preposition

We know that a preposition should not end a sentence or a clause. "*Who* are you looking for?" should be "*For whom* are you looking?" "What book does that passage come *from*?" should be "*From what* book does that passage come?".

But let us not forget Churchill's very firm and ponderous protest against the re-positioning of one of his prepositions in reply to one of his succinct memoranda—"This is an insult up with which I will not put." So perhaps, thanks to Churchill, we cannot be too dogmatic about this rule.

6. The Unrelated Relative Pronoun

This is perhaps one of the most common of all errors of syntax. Remember that the relative pronoun must have an antecedent; therefore, give it one or recast the sentence. For example—

> They could not find a quorum to hold a meeting *which* meant it had to be cancelled.

Here the relative pronoun *which* has no antecedent. The sentence must therefore be re-cast in some way—

> They could not find a quorum to hold a meeting, and, because of this, the meeting had to be cancelled.

Or—

> They could not find a quorum to hold a meeting; this meant it had to be cancelled.

7. The Present Participle and the Gerund

It is sometimes difficult to recognize their difference; but you should note that the present participle is a verbal adjective, whereas the gerund is a verbal noun. Look at these sentences—

> I did not see the man *approaching*.

Approaching is a present participle, that is to say, a verbal adjective, telling us something more about the word "man."

> I knew nothing about him *planning* the holiday.

Planning is a verbal noun or gerund; therefore it must be governed by *his* the possessive adjective, so that the sentence now reads—

> I knew nothing about *his* planning the holiday.

8. Misrelated Participles

Always be careful when you use the present or past participle in opening a sentence. Used wrongly they can lead to strange oddities of speech. Remember that the participle must extend the subject of the sentence. For example—

> *Jumping* on the moving bus, *the old man* missed the step and was dragged along the street.

This is the correct use of the opening participle. The word *jumping* extends or describes the subject *the old man*.

Here are some examples of misrelated participles.

> *Walking* through the town, *the streets* looked deserted.

This is of course wrong, as it suggests that the streets were walking through the town. Correct it by changing the subject.

> *Walking* through the town, *we* found the streets deserted.

Can you spot the error in the following sentence?

> *Seated* in the train, *the time* seemed to us to pass almost too quickly.

Time was not of course actually sitting in the train! We can make sense of the sentence by turning the participial phrase into a subordinate clause.

> As we sat in the train, the time seemed to us to pass almost too quickly.

N.B. You can often correct a misrelated participle by turning the sentence upside down. For instance—

Being a fine day, we went to a picnic.

This can be corrected as follows—

The day being fine, we went for a picnic.

9. "Shall" and "Will"

These two auxiliary or helping verbs which indicate future tense, are conjugated in this way—

	Singular	*Plural*
First Person	I shall	We shall
Second Person	Thou wilt	You will
Third Person	He, she, it will	They will

Used like this, they indicate simple futurity; but, to indicate something more emphatic than intention, to convey the idea of purpose and determination, command or threat, we reverse their conjugation, as follows—

	Singular	*Plural*
First Person	I will	We will
Second Person	Thou shalt	You shall
Third Person	He, she, it shall	They shall

"I *shall* be there" is a simple promise of future intention; but "I *will* be there" indicates my intention to allow nothing to prevent my attendance. "They *will* follow us to the station" is a statement of what is expected; but "They *shall* follow us" expresses a threat of rebuke in case of failure to follow. "Thou *shalt* not steal" is a command, very different from "Thou *wilt* not steal."

N.B. In questions, *shall* and *will* carry fine distinctions of meaning—

"*Shall* we go?" means "Do you wish us to go?"
"*Will* you go?" means "Do you intend to go?"
"*Shall* you go?" means "Is there any likelihood of your going?"
"*Will* she go?" means "Is it likely she will go?"

10. "Should" and "Would"

"Should" normally replaces "shall," and "would" replaces "will" when the past tense is used.

We do not say "I *shall* be glad if you *would* do this," but "I *shall* be glad if you *will* do this" or "I *should* be glad if you *would* do this." "We shall be glad if you will" is used when a request is being made for something which we have a right to expect, e.g.—

  (a) We shall be glad if you will let us have your cheque without further delay.
  (b) We shall be glad if you will replace the damaged furniture before the end of the week.

"We should be glad if you would (or could)" is used when a favour is being asked, e.g.—

  (a) We should be glad if you would let us know whether they pay accounts promptly.
  (b) We should be glad if you could reduce your quotation in view of the competition we have to face.

N.B. Should is used for all three persons when duty or obligation is implied, e.g. "He *should* accept the result, but I cannot say whether he will."

11. "May" and "Can"

Very often *can* is used wrongly instead of *may*.
Can means simply ability to do.
May implies permission.

  "Can I bring John back to tea?" should be—
  "May I bring John back to tea?"

Can is properly used in this sentence—

  "Can you lift this table?"

EXERCISE

Correct the following sentences and give reasons for your corrections.

  1. I have only spoken to him once.
  2. Soldiers are trained to quickly obey orders.
  3. They said that they had and would again call on him.

4. This house is the most commodious of the two, but any of them would suit us.
5. Talking at such a rate, the subject was too involved for me to grasp easily.
6. Is this amount to be subtracted or added to the total?
7. Girls required for picking fruit fifteen years old.
8. I hoped to have gone with you to the party but, between you and I, I could not afford the time.
9. He said it was us who had been responsible for him not coming to the meeting.
10. He neither admitted that his action was wrong or that it had caused annoyance to others.
11. Checking the figures carefully, the clerk's mistake was soon discovered by the inspector.
12. I cannot sing like I used to.
13. The secretary is a man whom I know is reliable.
14. I am determined that this item will be discussed.
15. Each of the committee were in favour of him being appointed secretary.
16. One should always count your blessings.
17. This rack is only to be used for light articles.
18. Though not wishing to insist upon it, this point deserves consideration.
19. He shall be taking his seat on the board next week.
20. I should like to have seen them again before I leave.
21. This law will not only affect the poor but the rich.
22. Either of the four red pencils and any of the two pens will do.
23. Should you say that this quotation is good or merely fair?
24. This collection of pens, pencils and books are cluttering up my desk.
25. He asked the gatekeeper if he could enter the building.
26. It all depends now on them coming in time.
27. Neither of them were prepared for the emergency.
28. The committee are divided in their view.
29. Please tell me if I can take my holiday in June.
30. The fire spread quickly to the next building which caused immediate panic.

–6–

Accuracy of Expression

In all writing accuracy of expression is important. It is a good idea to cultivate a wide and accurate vocabulary, adding to it new words when opportunity occurs, but be on your guard against using such words solely for effect; for this will only result in stilted and awkward expression.

Whenever you come across an unfamiliar word, refer to a dictionary and memorize the exact meaning of the word, its correct pronunciation and its part of speech so that you will know how to use the word properly.

Remember that words are the means by which we seek to influence the minds of others—to convince, to persuade, to encourage, to dissuade. They are powerful instruments when used correctly. Used incorrectly, they make fools of us.

Synonyms

The dictionary gives this definition: "one or two more words having the same or nearly the same essential meaning." For example—

>   grand, majestic   task, work, duty
>   battle, conflict   acute, keen, sharp
>   amiable, lovable   state, realm, condition

Sometimes we find pairs of words that seem identical in meaning, but closer examination reveals a distinction not at first apparent, e.g. wealthy, rich.

ACCURACY OF EXPRESSION

"Wealthy" is applied to a person "having great possessions," "owning wealth." "Rich," while indicating "wealth," may also be applied to the following, though with a different meaning in each instance—

rich soil	fertile soil
rich food	full of nutritive ingredients
rich quality	superior quality

It is obvious therefore that you must be careful in your use of synonyms. With the aid of a dictionary study the following synonyms and note that in some cases the words have a secondary meaning—

achieve, accomplish, perform, gain
adept, proficient, skilled
conformity, likeness, similarity
contingency, accident, chance
exigency, emergency, necessity
eminent, distinguished, conspicuous
illicit, unlawful, unlicensed
insidious, treacherous, false, cunning
vacillate, hesitate, waver

Antonyms

These are words of opposite meaning. For example—

good and *bad*	*genuine* and *false*
white and *black*	*joy* and *sorrow*
guilt and *innocence*	*extravagant* and *thrifty*

Homonyms

A homonym is a word having the same pronunciation as another but differing from it in origin, meaning and, often, in spelling. For example—

bare and *bear*	*meet* and *meat*
pail and *pale*	*site* and *cite*
dear and *deer*	*maid* and *made*

N.B. It may help you to remember the different meanings of synonym, antonym, and homonym if you know of their Greek derivation.

onym	name
syn	with
anti	against
homo	same

Pairs of Words

Learn to differentiate between words that look alike or sound alike; close observation, practice and the use of your dictionary is the only way to master them. Here are some—

adverse	averse
affect	effect
comprehensive	comprehensible
contiguous	contagious
council	counsel
credulity	credibility
depreciate	deprecate
illegible	eligible
principle	principal

EXERCISE I

1. Give antonyms for—general, smooth, ugly, aristocratic, masterful, prone, propitious.
2. Use the following homonyms in sentences to show their differences in meaning—ranker, rancour; serial, cereal; bough, bow.
3. Explain the difference between—practice and practise; dependent and dependant; intervene and interfere; disinterested and uninterested; continuous and continual.

Misused Words

"Awful"

We are all too often guilty of the misuse of this word.

> April was an *awful* month.
> John really is an *awful* ass.
> Daphne was an *awful* sight in that hat.

We should only be justified in describing weather as *awful* if we were witnessing a severe thunderstorm which, in fact, seemed to threaten life and property and so fill us with *awe*. No person foolish enough to be described as an ass can create a feeling of awe! *Awful* therefore is legitimately used in reference to a catastrophe such as the destruction wrought by an earthquake or a tidal wave. The burning at the stake of a martyr must indeed have been an *awful* spectacle; but Daphne in her new hat could not possibly be an *awful* sight.

"Nice"

This is another word which is so over-worked that it has now lost meaning. Therefore avoid using it in any way other than correctly, namely—

> Francis has a *nice* ear for music

Here *nice* means "discriminating."

> That is much too *nice* a distinction to make.

Here nice means "subtle" or "delicate."

"Infer" and "Imply"

These two words are often misused because we are not aware of their proper meanings. *Infer* means "to form an opinion," "to come to a conclusion." It is therefore incorrect to say "Are you *inferring* that I don't know what I'm talking about?" The correct word to use in this instance is *implying*. *Imply* means "to hint," "to suggest."

These words are correctly used in the following sentences—

> Your letter seems to *imply* (suggest) that we have given the wrong advice.

> We can only *infer* (gather the impression) that you are not anxious to accept our terms.
>
> Your *inference* is correct; the man was in fact discharged for dishonesty.
>
> Such an *implication* is quite unjustifiable; we have not the slightest intention of misleading you.

"Anticipate"

Anticipate means "to forestall," "to be beforehand with," as in—

> Your letter of the 19th has *anticipated* an inquiry we were on the point of sending you.

"Appreciate"

Good wine, furniture, and violins *appreciate* with age. In other words they "increase in value" whereas clothing, property, and machinery *depreciate* as they grow older. However, we often use the word *appreciate* in the sense of welcome which is wrong.

> We *appreciate* their influence for good in public life.

This is correct in the sense that we give them credit for their integrity and public spirit; but to say "We *appreciated* their visit at Easter" is to use the word loosely.

"Disinterested"

We frequently confuse *disinterested* with *uninterested*. To be *disinterested* in a matter is to be without self-interest in it, to be impartial and detached. To be *uninterested* is to have no interest. The umpire at a cricket match should be disinterested. If he were uninterested he might fall asleep and be unable to do his job.

The above are examples of some of the words we are apt to misuse. Be on the look out for others and when you do come across them, check them in your dictionary and learn their correct use.

Idiomatic use of Prepositions

We are sometimes very careless in our use of prepositions with words. Too often we say accompanied *with* instead of *by*, or different *to* when it should be different *from*.

ACCURACY OF EXPRESSION

Here, to help you, is a list of words and their correct prepositions.

> agree *with* a person
> agree *to* a proposal or plan
> averse *to* a plan or suggestion
> collaborate *with* a person
> comply *with* a request
> consequent *upon* an action
> correspond *with* a person
> correspond *to* (one thing may correspond *to* another)
> deficient *in* knowledge, etc.
> defer *to* a person's viewpoint or wish
> distaste *for* an action, situation or thing
> entrust *to* a person
> entrust *with* a thing
> indifferent *to* criticism, a person or situation
> impatient *with* a person
> impatient *of* authority, control
> negligent *of* duty
> responsible *for* an action
> responsible *to* a person
> relevant *to* a discussion, point of view
> preferable *to* a person or thing
> prevail *upon* (*on*) a person
> substitute *for* a person or thing

Learn to use your prepositions correctly.

EXERCISE II

1. Compose sentences illustrating the slightly different senses in which the following words are used—

    confounded, confused, involved, complicated

2. Find a synonym to replace each of the following—
    (*a*) not loud enough to be heard
    (*b*) siding neither with one side nor the other
    (*c*) on the spur of the moment
    (*d*) severely simple
    (*e*) a person who shows great kindness to others

(f) an addition to a will
(g) moderation in eating or drinking
(h) a person's life-story written by himself

3. Show in a sentence the preposition(s) to be used after the following—

   affinity, abstain, compensate, responsible, instil, essential

4. These words have a correct use though they are more often used loosely or colloquially, Write two sentences for each of the following words, one to show its incorrect use, the other to show its correct use.

   nice, frightful, dreadful, hopeless

5. The following words are similar in sound; explain the difference of meaning in each case—
   (a) *advice* and *advise*
   (b) *compliment* and *complement*
   (c) *horde* and *hoard*
   (d) *plane* and *plain*
   (e) *session* and *cession*

6. Write down the nouns from the following words. (For the first two words there are two possible nouns.)

   announce, pronounce, denounce, renounce

–7–

A Business-like Style

It is not quite enough, when writing business letters, merely to be able to spell and punctuate correctly. There is the matter of style to be considered. What exactly do we mean by style?

Essentially, style could be said to be suitability, the suitability of the words to the object or occasion. Since we would not describe the scenery in business letters, extensive use of adjectives would be out of place. Be business-like when writing business letters! That is to say, be clear, concise, and polite. I have made a list of hints which may help you to achieve a business-like tone in your letters.

1. Use the concrete word, not the abstract.
2. Prefer the short word to the long word.
3. Do not use more words than necessary.
4. Prefer the familiar word.
5. Cultivate the transitive verb.
6. Guard against the over-use of adjectives.
7. Prefer the active to the passive voice.

Here are some common errors which you would do well to avoid.

AMBIGUITY. The Oxford English Dictionary gives this definition: "Double meaning; expression capable of more than one meaning." A few examples will help to illustrate this—

Sandra told Linda that her mother was ill.
The manageress said to her assistant that the fault was hers.
The typewriter needed repairing badly.

Ambiguity often arises from the use of involved and over-long sentences, the careless use of pronouns (particularly third personal pronouns), phrases or words misplaced, and weak punctuation. Clear thinking before writing, therefore, is essential.

CLICHÉ. This is a hackneyed phrase or expression. The constant use of cliché produces staleness both in speech and writing. In your letters, avoid clichés. Some of the more common of these are—

> be that as it may; in well-informed circles; conspicuous by its absence; far be it from me to; at the parting of the ways; the psychological moment; leave no stone unturned; in any shape or form; last but not least; shrewd suspicion; it stands to reason; strange as it may seem; needless to say; no shadow of doubt.

COLLOQUIALISM. It is difficult at times to differentiate between slang and colloquialism. The latter is the use of words, phrases or expressions acceptable in familiar or popular speech, but which are not suitable in formal speech or writing. Try to avoid colloquialisms in your business letters. Some examples are—

> quite all right; to go all out; in the soup; couldn't care less; where on earth?

The colloquial forms, *she'd*, *don't*, *he'll*, *I'll*, etc., although used in ordinary conversation, are not used in formal writing except in direct quotation or dialogue.

N.B. Colloquialisms are not necessarily always bad English. But in a business letter they give the impression that the writer is being slack or lazy, and this is discourteous.

SLANG. These are words, expressions, phrases in common colloquial use, but unacceptable in standard English. In another sense, they are peculiar to or used in some special sense by a class or group of people, by a trade or profession. For example, a schoolboy talks of *swotting*, *cribbing*, a *grind*, *prep.*, etc. And the Armed Forces have their own language of slang, e.g., the R.A.F. talk of *prang*, *wizard*, *bus*, etc.

A BUSINESS-LIKE STYLE 47

A host of slang expressions has found its way into our familiar speech. Here are a few—

> tight as a drum; to go off the deep end; to give the O.K.; to get a kick out of; to tick off; scram; fed-up with; browned off.

There are many others and you should be constantly on guard against introducing any into letters of business. They both cheapen and weaken the language.

COMMERCIAL JARGON. There is no special language for business. Some textbooks have in fact tended to encourage the idea that business calls for some kind of separate language. In my opinion it does not. (see Chapter 9).

Modern business practice has happily done away with the ponderous and stilted mode of expression so prevalent only a few years ago. Writing for business today calls primarily for clarity and brevity. The old-fashioned *We beg to acknowledge receipt of* has at last died, replaced by the simple *Thank you for your letter* or *We have received your letter. Ult., Inst., prox.* may still linger on in places, but in your letters you should most certainly abandon them.

Commercial jargon, sometimes called *commercialese*, is not always easy to recognize, but be on a constant look out for it. It tends to creep into your letters, no matter how careful you are. At least you can try to avoid the more obvious horrors of commercial jargon. Listed here are some of them. Alongside each, in italics, is a simple and straight-forward translation for use in your letters.

It has been brought to our notice	*We note* or *We notice*
I am wholly at a loss to understand	*I cannot understand*
It will be our earnest endeavour	*We shall try*
Enclosed please find *or* We enclose herewith	*We enclose*
We are of the opinion that	*We think that*
We wish to acquaint you	*We have to inform you*

in view of the fact that	*because of*
Your good selves	*You*
at your earliest convenience	*as soon as possible*
I have instituted the necessary inquiries	*I am inquiring*
It is within our power	*We can*
We are prepared to offer	*We offer*
downward movement in prices	*fall in prices*
Your order to hand	*We have received your order*
It is incumbent upon me	*I must*

Omit from your vocabulary *we beg to remain*, anything *to hand* and *oblige*. There are others, not so obvious perhaps, often of the single word variety, such as *commence* when you mean *begin*, or *advise* when you mean *inform*.

Communication is such a long way of saying *letter* or *inquiry*.

Send is so much simpler than *dispatch*, and *anticipate* is too often used when you mean simply *expect*.

Moreover, do try to avoid using that ridiculous word *same*, e.g. "We thank you for *same*." It simply means, *the matter*, or *the problem* or *your inquiry* depending on what it is you are referring to. Say exactly what you mean!

Always try to use the simplest word and so give your letter a business-like clarity. One final word of warning; beware of using new jargon. I am thinking of the cult of *wise*—financial*wise*, tax*wise*, etc. As with the old, keep new jargon out of your letters.

REDUNDANCY. This is the use of unnecessary words. For example—

The shop assistant restored the umbrella *back* to its owner.

Restored means *give back*, so that in this example the same thing is being said twice. Therefore the word *back* is redundant in the sentence and should be omitted.

He was *often* in the habit of going to the races.

Here the word *often* means the same as *in the habit of* and is therefore redundant.

A BUSINESS-LIKE STYLE

EXERCISE

Write these sentences in concise and clear English, giving reasons for your corrections.

1. The one is equally as bad as the other.
2. The boss went off the deep end when I told him.
3. Economically, this country is up against it.
4. He said to John that the responsibility was his.
5. We learn from well-informed circles that now is the psychological moment to show just where we stand; now is the time when no stone must be left unturned if we are to achieve our aim.
6. Give me the O.K. when you are ready.
7. You must come to a final conclusion.
8. Come up to the front of the room.
9. It will be our earnest endeavour to execute your order at the very earliest opportunity.
10. Without exception we decided unanimously to adopt the proposal.
11. Those who had been so anxious to call the meeting were, when it came to the crunch, conspicuous by their absence.
12. The reason why the estimate was low was because they were anxious to land the contract.
13. In the light of experience it is my opinion that the escalation of prices will continue for some considerable time.
14. He sent in his notice because he was browned off with the office set-up.
15. We beg to acknowledge receipt of your letter of 10th inst., in which you furnish us with details of your inquiries.

–8–

Planning a Business Letter

In this chapter we deal with the lay-out or framework of a business letter and its component parts. It is important to remember that very often your letter is the first contact you have with a firm. It is essential therefore that it creates a good impression, both in lay-out and content.

Let us look at the letter head, which is normally specially printed. It contains the firm's name, address, telex and telephone numbers, departmental references, name of manager, board of directors, etc. Here are a few examples—

Harris & Bowen Ltd *Building Contractors*

Tel: 041–332 1070/1   70–78 Bath Square
Branch Manager R. A. Thomson   Glasgow C2

Carfax National Building Society

---

12 Prince Street, Edinburgh EH2 1JB Tel: 031–661 2417
General Manager T. S. Mead FCIS
Your Ref   Our ref

Lowland Malt Distillers Limited

Directors: T. M. Smith (Chairman) W. V. Hannah, J. K. R. Black

Export Department

Telephone 041-258 4018   68 Waterloo Street
Telegrams Madis Glasgow   Glasgow C2

Let us now study in detail the lay-out of a business letter (see page 52). The key to the framework is as follows—

(1) Date
(2) Reference
(3) Inside Address
(4) Salutation
(5) Subject-heading
(6) Body of letter
(7) Complimentary Ending
(8) Signature and Conclusion
(9) Enclosure(s)

We shall discuss each of these in turn.

(1) DATE. This should be typed in full, normally in the order of day, month, year, as in—

15 November 19—

Modern tendency is to omit commas. The day of the week may also be included, preferably on a separate line. The general appearance is then better if the year is moved to a line of its own, e.g.—

Tuesday
15 November
19—

(2) REFERENCE LETTERS. In basic form these are the initials of the dictator followed by those of the typist, e.g.—

Our Ref FM/RS

Sometimes a file number is added, as in—

Our Ref FM/RS/107

Harris & Bowen Ltd *Building Contractors*

Tel: 041-332 1070/1 70-78 Bath Square
Branch Manager R. A. Thomson Glasgow C2

(2)...................... (1)......................

(3)...
....
....

(4)...................................

        (5)...................................

(6) ....
....
....
....

....
....
....

....
....
....

           (7)...................................
           ....

                (8)...................................

(9)...................................

The key to this framework is on page 51.

There may be other references, to an account number or to a client's number; these should be quoted in your reply, e.g.—

Our Ref FM/RS
Your Ref 583/P

The purpose of reference letters and numbers is to enable rapid identification of correspondence to be made.

(3) INSIDE ADDRESS. This is the name and address of the person to whom the letter is being sent. It may be in *block* form, as in—

W. A. Menzies & Co Ltd
43 Newton Street
Edinburgh 8

or in *indented* form, as in—

W. A. Menzies & Co Ltd
   43 Newton Street
      Edinburgh 8

If at all possible the address should be confined to three or four lines. If necessary, the name of a town and county may be included in one line, e.g.—

The Secretary
Nu-Lino Company
41 King Street
Preston, Lancs

Note carefully the use of *Messrs*. It should be used when addressing a partnership, as in—*Messrs* Smith & Moodie; *Messrs* W. Black & Company.

Note, however, that *Messrs* should not be used when writing to a limited company; your letter should be addressed to The Secretary or some other official of the company, e.g. General Manager, Manager, Accountant, etc.

Where firms are known by a simple trading name, even although personal, do not use *Messrs*, e.g. Boots, Timothy White. Also, do not add *Messrs* to the impersonal, e.g. Royal Friendly Society; and where the name of a firm contains a conferred title, the addition of *Messrs* would be quite out of place, e.g. Sir Isaac Pitman & Sons Ltd.

Letters for the attention of. Practice here varies, but you should keep to the formal procedure and set out your letter like this—

Smith & Jones Ltd
14 High Street
Carlisle

For the attention of Mr Thomas

Dear Sirs,

Note that the impersonal *Dear Sirs* is used because you are, in fact, addressing your letter to the company.

(4) SALUTATION. The normal form of this in business correspondence is—

Dear Sir(s) or *Dear Madam (Mesdames)*

There are, however, two further forms of salutation to be considered—

(i) *Sir, Gentlemen, Madam, Mesdames* These are used in more formal correspondence, namely, official reports and government correspondence, etc.

(ii) *Dear Mr (Mrs/Miss), Dear . . .* This form permits the only use of *Yours sincerely* in business letters and is used only when the person addressed is known by the writer. But firms may have their own rules about this practice.

N.B. There are, of course, special forms of address, e.g. to nobility, the clergy, etc. These are listed in any good dictionary.

(5) SUBJECT-HEADING. In business letters this is used to give prominence to the subject matter, as in this example.

Dear Sir,

Harold John Stewart

This young man has applied to us for a post in our Advertising Department. He states that . . .

Remember that the subject-heading should be underlined.

(6) BODY OF LETTER. This is obviously the most important section of any business letter. There are rules of style which, if followed, give point and clarity to the message in the letter; these are discussed in detail in Chapter 9. Here we are concerned only with the basic guides of presentation of material.

The subject-matter should be written in concise and clear English. Spelling must be accurate. Care should be taken not to over-punctuate.

Normally each item in the letter should be given a separate paragraph. Sometimes this may consist of a single sentence. But beware of too many short paragraphs for these tend to spoil the appearance of a letter. Note also that a letter, unless very short, should never be written in one paragraph.

You should avoid the use of abbreviations other than accepted ones. Be careful in your use of the *ampersand* (&) for *and:* it should not be used in the body of the letter except (*a*) in reference to a firm, e.g. Brown & Company, and (*b*) when referring to numbers, e.g. pages 10 & 11.

It is becoming the fashion nowadays for more and more firms to use the fully-blocked open-punctuated form of letter. The O and M Section of the Civil Service Department have come out in favour of it and have produced evidence to show that between 10 and 20 per cent of total typewriting time may be saved by using this style. Many Government Departments are taking up the style also.

Some of the letters in this book are fully-blocked and have open punctuation. So the easiest way for you to understand what is meant by the term is simply to take a look at one of the examples of different kinds of Business Letter in the following chapter. Look at the letter on page 61, for instance. You will find that "fully-blocked" describes the shape of paragraphs which are blocked from the left-hand margin rather than indented in the first line. When a paragraph ends we move down 2 line spaces and begin again at the left hand margin.

"Open punctuation" means the complete omission of all punctuation (except in the body of the letter) that can be omitted without risk of ambiguity.

The style is accompanied by a number of other devices that aid speed and economy without reducing clarity and legibility. For example 1730 hrs is written rather than 5.30 pm. Eg is typed for "for example" or etc for "et cetera."

Given a clear-cut type-face and even block typing with adequate white space between paragraphs so that eye and mind are not confounded, the fully-blocked, open-punctuated style is aesthetically pleasing as well as economical.

(7) COMPLIMENTARY ENDING. It is important to note that this should conform with the Salutation as follows—

Dear Sir/Madam	Yours faithfully
Dear Mr Jones	
Dear Jones	Yours sincerely
Dear Robert	

Yours truly or *Yours very truly* is sometimes used in place of *Yours sincerely*, when the relationship may not be so personal.

Note the more formal endings—

Sir/Gentlemen	Your obedient servant
Madam/Mesdames	Yours respectfully

The use of *I remain*, placed before the ending, is out-moded and should be avoided.

(8) SIGNATURE AND CONCLUSION. The name of the firm is normally typed immediately below the Complimentary Ending, allowing sufficient space for signature. Many signatures to business letters are illegible; when this is the case, a sensible practice is to type the name in brackets under the signature.

If the firm title is used, whether written, typed or rubber-stamped, the person signing should add his initials. In more formal cases the following form is adapted—

Per pro   Metropolitan Insurance Co
            John E Howard
            Secretary

PLANNING A BUSINESS LETTER

Note these examples of signatures—

Sole trader	Arthur Brand
Partnership	May Banks & Co
Limited Company	For King, Miles & Co Ltd,
	John Grant
	Director
Local Authority	Newcastle Urban District Council
	Roger Caird
	Clerk to the Council

Each member of a Partnership signs in the style adopted by the firm, as—

> May Banks & Co
>
> ————————
>
> Partner

In the case of a Limited Company the official who signs may be the Director, Accountant, Secretary, Sales Manager or other official concerned with the matter in question.

Per pro or pp is an abbreviation for the Latin words *per procurationem*, indicating that the signatory has signed for and on behalf of the company with full authority.

Persons who are authorized to conduct correspondence for their firm, but who have not been given power of procuration, sign as follows—

for (or pp) May Banks & Co   or   May Banks & Co
            R. Baird   Per R.B.

(9) ENCLOSURE(s). These are shown by the abbreviation *Enc.* or 2 *Encs.*, etc., typed at the bottom left-hand margin.

There are other ways of indicating enclosures—(*a*) by a stick-on enclosure slip on which is written the number of enclosures, (*b*) by a solidus (/) typed in the margin opposite the reference to the enclosure in the letter itself, (*c*) three dashes(- - -) typed in the margin opposite the reference to the enclosure in the letter.

N.B. In these sections we have explained the component parts of a business letter. There may be some variations to the above framework, but they will only be slight.

Remember what we said at the beginning of this chapter—that frequently the only contact you may have with a company or firm is by letter. Therefore, perfection in letter-writing becomes an essential.

In the next chapter we discuss the more routine types of business letters, and give numerous examples. Study these carefully.

–9–

Different Types of Business Letter

Below are listed some guide-lines which may help you to write good business letters.

BE ACCURATE. The information you convey in a business letter must be accurate. Therefore, make sure that any facts and figures given are correct.

THINK CLEARLY. Reflect before you write so that the meaning conveyed in your letter will be clear, both to you and to the recipient.

WRITE SIMPLY. This should follow naturally from clear thinking, but too often complexities arise from the written word, and generally, this stems from an artificial style. Get into the habit of using short words, short sentences and short paragraphs; this makes a letter quick and easy to read. It will also be easier to understand.

BE BRIEF. This means that you should exercise an economy of words; it does not mean that you have to be abrupt. In business no one wants to read extraneous or superfluous matter. It is a waste of time. But be sure, in your economy, that you have made your meaning clear.

BE POSITIVE. This does not mean being dogmatic; it means simply that you should follow a positive rather than a negative approach. Such an approach adds clarity and point to your letter. Where possible, prefer the active to the passive voice.

BE COURTEOUS. It is important, when writing business letters, to maintain a courteous manner. Business may be lost on account of a rude or slovenly letter. The company or firm to which you are writing will form its opinion of your company or firm by judging not only the facts in your letter, but also its general tone. Try reading your letter aloud. Does it *sound* pleasant?

So you must learn to produce letters that are neatly set out and well presented, free from errors and jargon. In this way you create a favourable image for your firm. A poor letter, badly presented, no matter how important its matter may be, only irritates and does nothing to help a firm's business.

Cherish this as your golden rule—*Never let a letter go without being satisfied with it.*

Now study the letter on the page opposite. Does it follow the rules above? It is accurate and clear; it is simple and brief; it is positive and courteous. It does therefore follow the guide lines suggested.

PLASTICHROME & CO LTD

Directors:
H. Morton
J. A. Blakey
T. Y. Thomson

Highfield Works
Wolverhampton WV6 8DW

Ref SD 181
JW/EB

Messrs Stone & Goldie
21 Bridge Street
Manchester MI4 4P6   1 September, 19..

Dear Sirs

We have pleasure in enclosing our receipt for your cheque for £36.

You were quite right to deduct the discount of ten per cent, according to the special arrangements made with you when the order was placed.

We thank you for your order received today and are pleased to inform you that the goods will be dispatched in about ten days' time to meet your requirements.

Yours faithfully
PLASTICHROME & CO LTD
John H Wright
(Sales Manager)

EXERCISE 1

1. Write replies to the following classified advertisements—
   (a) LABRABOXER PUPPIES for sale. Sweet-tempered Boxer mother, handsome Labrador father. Any reasonable offer accepted for sake of good homes. Rose Cottage, Green Lane, Bromley, BR2 0HJ.
   (b) HI-FI £200 radiogram/tape-recorder for £65. Top make. New, unused. Thorne, 40 Richmond Place, Chiselhurst BR7 6DA
2. Write a letter to a seaside hotel inquiring about holiday accommodation.
3. Write a letter to your local College of Further Education inquiring about secretarial courses.
4. As club secretary write a letter to a club member who has not been at a club meeting for some time.
5. As secretary to a Headmaster draft a letter to parents inviting them to the school play during the Christmas holidays.

QUOTATIONS

The first step in a business transaction is usually an inquiry about prices, range of goods, availability of goods, etc. To enable the buyer to discover new sources of supply or to obtain details of quality and price, he sends inquiries to several firms. He will receive in return a quotation.

When submitting a quotation, the following points should be noted—

(a) A clear description of the goods offered must be given. Where possible, samples should be sent.
(b) Prices and terms should be given. Discounts, if any, should be shown.
(c) Delivery-terms should be stated, e.g. carriage paid or carriage forward.
(d) If there is a limiting period, then this should be indicated, e.g. subject to acceptance within fourteen days.

Here is an example of a letter of inquiry; on the next page there is the quotation sent in reply.

```
              THOMSON  &  SON  LIMITED
                    16 Gordon Street
                      Glasgow C2

1 March 19..

Border Tweeds Ltd
Kelso

Dear Sirs

We shall be pleased to know if you can supply us with Tweed lengths
suitable for skirt-making, also your prices and terms.

It would be helpful if you could supply samples.

Yours faithfully
for Thomson & Son Ltd
James Kerr

Ref: JK/RS
```

**Border Tweeds Ltd
Kelso**

Your ref: JK/RS

Our ref: RT/IM
Thomson & Son Ltd
16 Gordon Street
Glasgow C2   6th March 19..

Dear Sirs

  Thank you for your inquiry of 1st March.
We can supply the following Tweed
lengths from present stock:

```
Shade No 32 in 40 yd lengths @   99p per yd
Shade No 38 in 30 yd lengths @ £1·15 per yd
Shade No 47 in 30 yd lengths @   89p per yd
Shade No 58 in 60 yd lengths @   75p per yd
Shade No 63 in 30 yd lengths @ £1·15 per yd
```

  All are suitable for skirt-making; samples
of each are enclosed.
  Terms are 5% discount (7 days), $2\frac{1}{2}$%
(30 days), carriage forward.
  We hope that you will place an order
with us.

                        Yours faithfully
                        for Border Tweeds Ltd
                        Ron Turner
Encs   (Manager)

ORDER LETTERS

When ordering goods, care must be taken to state requirements clearly so that the seller will have no difficulty in dispatching the exact goods asked for. It should never be necessary for him to refer to former orders or to write for further details. If goods are ordered from a catalogue or numbered list, the clearest indication that can be given is to quote the catalogue or list number.

The date when delivery is desired should be stated, also the method of transport preferred—road, rail, sea or air.

The goods may be required at the office address or at the warehouse address of the firm; they may even be delivered direct to the address of a customer of the buyers. It is essential therefore to state *where* the goods are to be sent.

N.B. Remember that all relevant information should be given in an order letter. It is more business-like—and certainly it helps to prevent orders being misread—to tabulate the items required.

As a guide to the paragraphing of an order letter, we suggest you include—

    (*a*) reference to a source of information
    (*b*) list of goods to be ordered
    (*c*) quantity, quality, price, catalogue number (if any)
    (*d*) details of delivery and payment

On the next page you will find an example of a letter of this sort.

THOMSON & SON LIMITED
16 Gordon Street
Glasgow C2

10 March 19..

The Manager
Border Tweeds Ltd
Kelso

Dear Sir

Thank you for your quotation of 6 March, also for the samples of Tweed.

We shall be pleased if you will forward the following lengths:

6 - 40 yd lengths Tweed, Shade No 32 @ 99p per yd
3 - 30 yd lengths Tweed, Shade No 47 @ 89p per yd
3 - 60 yd lengths Tweed, Shade No 58 @ 75p per yd

by British Road Services to the above address.

Your terms are acceptable. Please deliver by 25 March as the Tweed is required to complete an urgent export order.

Yours faithfully
for Thomson & Son Ltd
James Kerr

Ref: JK/RS

Alternatively the order may be written on an Order Form and enclosed with a short letter as follows—

      T H O M S O N   &   S O N   L I M I T E D
         16 Gordon Street
          Glasgow C2

10 March 19..

The Manager
Border Tweeds Ltd
Kelso

Dear Sir

Thank you for your quotation of 6 March, also for the samples of Tweed.

We enclose our Order No 124 for material to be despatched to the above address by British Road Services.

Please deliver by 25 March as the Tweed is required to complete an urgent export order.

Yours faithfully
for Thomson & Son Ltd
James Kerr

Ref: JK/RS
enc

Here is another example.

Matthews Bros Ltd

164 Crow Road
York YO2 5DS

JR/MP/112

Petters Engineers
5 Hatton Street
Manchester M12 4NR   15 May 19..

Dear Sirs

Please forward to us at the above address
by Road Haulage the following machines:

3 Linear Portasaws
3 Smith water pumps
4 Bellview compressors

We wish delivery within one month, and ask
you also to clarify the guarantee and
servicing arrangements for these machines;
the order is subject to these being
acceptable.

Yours faithfully
for Matthews Bros Ltd
John Robertson
(General Manager)

ACKNOWLEDGMENTS

An order ought to be acknowledged by the seller; in this acknowledgment the following points should be included—(*a*) thanks for the order, (*b*) confirmation of details, (*c*) delivery-date, (*d*) courtesy-ending. Here and on the next page are two examples.

Jackson & Sons
51 Ralston Avenue,
Aberdeen AB1 8HQ

WM/MT

Messrs Smart & Sons
160 Crow Road
Bath BA5 3PY   14th June 19..

Dear Sirs

   Thank you for your order of 10th June for linen and silks. We have the goods in stock and shall dispatch them tomorrow by rail.

   You should therefore receive your order within seven days.

                      Yours faithfully
                      pp Jackson & Sons
                      W P Martin
                      (Textiles Manager)

**Border Tweeds Ltd
Kelso**

RT/IM

Thomson & Son Ltd
16 Gordon Street
Glasgow C2   13th March 19..

Dear Sirs

   Thank you for your letter of 10th March ordering the following material:

   6 – 40 yd lengths Tweed, Shade No 32
   3 – 30 yd lengths Tweed, Shade No 47
   3 – 60 yd lengths Tweed, Shade No 58

   We shall send the consignment to you on 17th March by British Road Services as requested.

   We trust you will find the Tweeds satisfactory and that we may receive further orders from you.

                    Yours faithfully
                    for Border Tweeds Ltd
                    Ron Turner
                    (Manager)

DIFFERENT TYPES OF BUSINESS LETTER

EXERCISE 11

Write appropriate letters from these notes—

1. Porteous Bros. 1 High Street, Glasgow C1 order the following goods from Meyrick & Co, 3 George Lane, Edinburgh EH3 1LY—

    2 kegs Californian honey
    1 drum Glycerine (re-distilled)

    Delivery is to be made by 20th March, by rail.

2. Meyrick & Co acknowledge the order, promising delivery as requested.

3. Heralds & Co, St Peter Port, Jersey, Channel Isles have received prices and patterns of carpets from Lord & Co, Wolverhampton, WV2 3HQ. They place this order—

    12 Wilton Carpets, size 12′ × 9′, colour No 3
    12 Axminster Carpets, size 12′ × 10′, colour No 7

    to be sent by Road Transport and by sea, fob. Delivery date—within one month.

4. Jones & Co, 4 Grange Street, Newcastle upon Tyne, NE2 3TL order a consignment of fruit from Noyes & Porter, 56 Weald Road, London E17 5LE. The fruit is to be sent by the Midlands Express Carrier Co, and is required by the end of the week. Noyes & Porter find that one item ordered cannot be forwarded as requested, as a shipment of that kind of fruit is not due until Saturday. Delivery of the other items is promised by the end of the week, and particulars are given regarding the completion of the order.

    Write the letter ordering the fruit; then write the acknowledgment.

5. Asplant & Son, 40 Bright Street, Coventry, CV6 7EQ send an order to Modern Plastics Ltd, 136 James Road, Liverpool L69 9AN for—

    20 dozen Plastic Containers No 8 as shown on p 4 of list.
    36 dozen Plastic Trays No 12 as shown on p 6 of list.

    to be sent by rail, delivery not later than 15 days.

    Write the letter ordering the goods and also the reply.

6. Write (*a*) an order for certain items of machinery. Ask for clarification of their guarantee and servicing arrangements.
   (*b*) an order in reply to a special offer, but ask for information regarding the possibility of repeat orders and the terms for these.
   (*c*) cancelling the order mentioned in (*a*); the machinery is not now required.

LETTERS OF COMPLAINT

It is sometimes necessary to make a complaint about the quality of goods received or about damage which has been done to them before they reached the buyer's premises. Late or incomplete delivery might also give rise to dissatisfaction.

Whatever may be the reason for complaint, annoyance must never be allowed to take precedence over courtesy. It should always be remembered that the sender of the goods may not be responsible for the condition about which complaint is made.

Damage done to the goods may be due to the carriers and not to the packing; delay in delivery may be traceable to the same cause or to a mistake in ordering. Delivery of goods not required or of insufficient goods may be the result of the buyer's carelessness in verifying the details of the order.

The following points should be embodied in a letter of complaint—

   (*a*) delivery of goods should be acknowledged
   (*b*) cause for complaint should be stated
   (*c*) request for action should be made
   (*d*) if necessary, replacement of goods should be asked for.

The following are examples of letters complaining about damaged goods.

MESSRS DAVIES & CO   89 Mill Lane
                               Black Pill
                               Swansea SA3 5BD
JH/DM/IB   4th April 19..
Messrs Garscube & Tomlin
20 Harrington Road
Bristol BS14 8LD

Dear Sirs,

   We received today the china ordered from
you on 28th March.

   Five crates are in perfect condition,
but in the sixth a large number of
breakages have occurred. The china appears
to have been carefully packed, as in the
case of the undamaged crates, and we
consider that the breakages may be the
result of careless handling by Railway
employees. Will you please make inquiries?

   We enclose a list of the goods damaged,
and shall be grateful if you will replace
these as soon as possible.

Yours faithfully,

James Hare
(Director)
Enc.

19 Mentone Terrace
Edinburgh EH9 1LY
9th January 19..

The Condé Publications Ltd
4 Bellevue Road
London SW5

Dear Sirs

As a regular subscriber to your magazine "Good Food," I was most disappointed to receive my January copy in such poor condition. The cover was torn and adrift from the magazine which had obviously been packed with no backing.

I shall be glad to receive a replacement, and trust that you will ensure that future copies sent to me will be suitably packaged.

Yours faithfully
Fraser Morton

N.B. a stronger, more decisive tone may be adopted if there has been a previous cause for complaint, but discourtesy is unnecessary and should be avoided.

Jackson & Sons
51 Ralston Avenue,
Aberdeen AB1 8HQ

AW/IP/105
Messrs Henderson Bros
105 Reid Street
Glasgow C2

3rd May 19..

Dear Sirs,

The three bales of silk to our order N.369 of 2nd April arrived today.

On examination we find them soiled at the edges because of torn outer wrappings. This is not the first time that we have had to make such a complaint about cloth received from you, and we must ask you to see that goods dispatched to us are more carefully packed.

The bales of silk are usable, but we suggest that you make us a reduction of 20 per cent on the price. Failing this, we shall have to return the bales.

Yours faithfully,
pp Jackson & Sons
Arthur White

Here is an example of a letter complaining about delay in delivery—

Hunt & Son
14 Percy Street, Newcastle Upon Tyne NE1 4PQ

PB/ST   4th June 19..
The Manager
Steel Cables Ltd
60 Alton Street
Coventry CV3 6NT

Dear Sir,

  On 15th May we ordered from you a consignment of Steel Cables for delivery by 31st May.

  As we have not yet received the Cables, we ask you to look into this matter and arrange their dispatch without further delay.

                           Yours faithfully
                           for Hunt & Son
                           Peter Bryce

REPLIES TO COMPLAINTS

In replying to a complaint about damaged goods, delay in delivery, etc., the seller should first of all express regret that the need for complaint has arisen. He should state what investigations have been made and where the blame appears to lie. If the buyer is responsible, then it is wise to admit this frankly.

Finally, the seller must suggest a remedy for the complaint—delayed goods must be forwarded, damaged goods must be replaced, etc.

Here, and on the next three pages, are some examples.

MESSRS. HALL & GOODE
21 Porter Street Hull HU1 2RG

JP/IH/47
Messrs Veitch & Co
84 Ventnor Road
London EC1 43H   17th December 19..

Dear Sirs,

Thank you for your letter of 15th December. I apologize for the non-delivery of the three Regal typewriters ordered by you. Our Packing Section had sent them in error to Hayes, Suffolk.

We are arranging to have the typewriters delivered by van on Thursday, as we know that you wish to have them before Christmas.

                    Yours faithfully
                    pp Hall & Goode
                    John Poole

Garscube & Tomlin Ltd

20 Harrington Road
Bristol BS14 8LD

HN/ST
Messrs Davies & Co
89 Mill Lane
Black Pill
Swansea SA3 5BD   8 April 19..

Dear Sirs

We much regret to learn from your letter of 4 April that the contents of one of the six crates of china received from us were badly damaged.

Our head packer informs us that all the crates were lined with our special shockproof packing, and that with reasonably careful handling no damage should have occurred. We are of course taking the matter up with the Railway Authorities.

We have sent off replacements to you today and trust that these will arrive in good condition.

> Yours faithfully
> Garscube & Tomlin Ltd
> Harvey Norris
> (Home Sales)

The Condé Publications Ltd

4 Bellevue Road
London SW5

14 January 19..

Fraser Morton Esq
19 Mentone Terrace
Edinburgh EH9 1LY

Dear Sir

Thank you for your letter of 9 January.
We are sorry to learn that you received
your copy of "Good Food" in such poor
condition.

We have now arranged to forward a
replacement copy properly packed, and have
taken the necessary steps to ensure that
future copies will reach you in perfect
condition.

Please accept our apology for the
inconvenience caused.

Yours faithfully
R O James
(Business Manager)

Steel Cables Ltd
60 Alton Street
Coventry CV3 6NT

JT/SR   7 June 19..
Messrs Hunt & Son
14 Percy Street
Newcastle upon Tyne NE1 4PQ

Dear Sirs

Thank you for your letter of 4 June. We much regret the delay in delivery of the Steel Cables ordered by you on 15 May.

A strike at the factory has held up production; the dispute however has been settled and we are now in a position to overtake our orders.

Your consignment has been dispatched today, and we trust the delay has not seriously inconvenienced you.

Yours faithfully
for Steel Cables Ltd
James Thorpe

DIFFERENT TYPES OF BUSINESS LETTER 81

EXERCISE III

Write suitable letters from the following notes—

1. (a) Seely & Co, Beresford Lane, Glasgow C2 write to Waters & Sons, 3 Crouch Corner, Sheffield S2 6BL complaining of damage done to two mahogany cabinets received. They are returning the damaged goods, and ask for immediate replacements.

   (b) Waters & Sons promise to replace the cabinets at once, but disclaim responsibility for damage. They state that the Railway Authorities have been informed.

2. (a) On 1st July, Carnie Bros, Peel Street, Southampton S01 1QU ordered from Primmer & Leeds, 14 Sefton Place, London W6 the following goods—

   3 doz Men's Drip-Dry Shirts (assorted) No 24.

   These were to be delivered by 10th July. On 13th July the goods have not arrived, and Carnie Bros, ask for information about them.

   (b) Primmer & Leeds have overlooked the order, owing to heavy pressure of business. They promise to send the goods immediately by Motor Express Co Ltd.

3. One ton Granulated Suger has been bought from Purdie & Sons, London N2, by Davidson Bros, 3 Carter Street, Nottingham NG1 7GG. The sugar is found on arrival to be of inferior quality and is damp. Purdie & Sons agree to replace it, as it is part of a new consignment which they have received and sent out unexamined.

   Write both the complaint and the reply.

4. Arnold Thin & Co of Bread Lane, Nottingham NG7 2RT, have ordered the following books from Smart's Publishing House, 52 The Wynd, Sheffield S1 2GA

   (a) 36 copies of "Electrical Who's Who"
   (b) 24 copies of "Electrical Resistance of Metals"
   (c) 6 copies of "The Electronic Trader"

   On delivery, 3 copies of (c) were missing. Payment is being held up meantime.

REQUESTS FOR PAYMENT

A first letter requesting payment of an account is generally very short. With it is enclosed the statement of account, and reference should be made to any terms of discount.

GARTON BROTHERS
22 Baker Road
Huddersfield HD3 3EX

24 May 19..

Messrs Tilden & Sprott
3 Grange Lane
York
YO2 5DS

Dear Sirs

We enclose statement of account for woollens ordered by you on 14 May.
A discount of 3 per cent is allowed on accounts settled within one month.

Yours faithfully
for Garton Brothers
Sydney Lamb

SL/MD/19
enc

If settlement is not made as a result of this letter, a further letter in more personal language should be sent when the discount period has elapsed. It is as well to remember that payment may be due to an oversight or to unbusinesslike methods of dealing with accounts. The customer should be reminded of the debt and of the fact that no discount can now be given. If there has been difficulty in obtaining the goods or in delivering them on the required date, or if a promise of payment by a certain date has not been kept, then it is advisable to bring these facts to the notice of the customer.

GARTON BROTHERS
22 Baker Road
Huddersfield HD3 3EX

24 June 19..

Messrs Tilden & Sprott
3 Grange Lane
York
YO2 5DS

Dear Sirs

We have to remind you that your account for woollens ordered on 14 May has not yet been met. Discount cannot now be allowed.

You will remember that we went to some trouble to help you in the matter of delivery by the stipulated date, and we are sure that you do not wish to inconvenience us by delaying payment.

A copy of the account is enclosed, and we shall be glad to receive your cheque.

Yours faithfully
for Garton Brothers
Sydney Lamb

SL/MD/19
enc

When the second request for payment does not bring settlement, it is possible that the customer is purposely witholding it. The tone of the next letter should be curt and pointed, but still courteous.

GARTON BROTHERS
22 Baker Road
Huddersfield HD3 3EX

8 September 19..

Messrs Tilden & Sprott
3 Grange Lane
York
YO2 5DS

Dear Sirs

Enclosed is the account for goods ordered on 14 May. This account is now long overdue. We shall be glad to have settlement without further delay.

Yours faithfully
for Garton Brothers
Sydney Lamb

SL/MD/19
enc

If persuasion and curtness have not had the desired result, legal proceedings, as a last resort, are threatened.

DIFFERENT TYPES OF BUSINESS LETTER 85

> GARTON BROTHERS
> 22 Baker Road
> Huddersfield HD3 3EX
>
> 12 December 19..
>
> Messrs Tilden & Sprott
> 3 Grange Lane
> York
> YO2 5DS
>
> Dear Sirs
>
> We regret to have to remind you that your May account is still outstanding. You will understand that we cannot wait indefinitely for settlement.
>
> If payment is not made within seven days we shall be compelled to instruct our solicitors to recover the amount outstanding.
>
> Yours faithfully
> for Garton Brothers
> Sydney Lamb
>
> SL/MD/19

EXERCISE IV

Write suitable letters from the following notes—

1. (*a*) Pickering & Quayle, 3 March Drive, Perth, send their account to Hamer & Co, 47 Clyde Street, Greenock. Terms—3 per cent discount on payment within one month.
   (*b*) Pickering & Quayle send their account for the second time. They remind Hamer & Co. of unfulfilled promise of payment.

(c) Pickering & Quayle threaten legal action if payment or part payment is not made within seven days.

2. (a) Bell & Co, 327 Mount Street, Brighton BN2 1PQ, request payment of an account of £60 from Peebles Bros, 146 Wilton Avenue, Portsmouth PO2 8LD. Peebles Bros are valued customers, and the delay in payment is probably due to an oversight.
   (b) Peebles Bros forward cheque with a letter of apology.

3. (a) Harper & Sons, 9 Queen Street, Brighouse, Yorkshire HD6 2RH have twice asked for settlement of the account of Davidson & Small, 129 Thayer Road, Hull HU9 4BN. They have to make up their books for the half-year, and wish payment of all outstanding accounts. Write their letter to Davidson & Small.
   (b) Davidson & Small apologize for delay in settling account. They state that they are experiencing difficulty in obtaining payment from customers. They promise to send cheque in a fortnight.
   (c) Harper & Sons agree to wait for a fortnight, but insist strongly on payment being made then.

4. Mr. Arthur Robson, 10 Lipton Street, Blackburn, Lancs BB6 7QJ, has not yet paid his account (£40) for last month. If he wishes to be allowed the usual $2\frac{1}{2}$ per cent discount, a remittance must be sent within three days.

5. (a) Messrs. Webster & Son, Beresford Street, Wembley, Middlesex HA0 1RU have made no payment against their debt of £66 outstanding for two months; until this amount has been cleared, no further orders can be accepted.
   (b) To the same firm ten days later. In the absence of any reply to the previous letter, warn them that it will be necessary to take legal measures. As they have been customers for several years, you would take such steps with regret, etc.

EXERCISE V

Supplying names, addresses and dates, write—
1. A letter enclosing account, mentioning terms of discount.
2. A persuasive letter when the discount period has elapsed.
3. A curt letter requesting immediate payment.
4. A letter threatening legal measures.

STATUS INQUIRIES

A firm which has never before dealt with us may be a little doubtful of our good faith when we send them an opening or first order. It is customary therefore, at the commencement of business relations, to give the name and address of at least one person or firm from whom reliable information about our business standing may be obtained. Alternatively, we may give the name of our bankers.

A letter written asking for information is called a *status inquiry*. Information is generally requested on the following points—

(a) The period of the firm's connection with the buyers.
(b) The frequency of orders received from them.
(c) The payment of accounts; discount allowed.
(d) The amount of credit to be allowed.

N.B. (a) and (b) are sometimes omitted, but (c) and (d) are vitally important.

The following two letters are examples of status inquiries requiring information of this sort.

THOMAS & CO
1 Greenbank Lane,
Blackpool FY1 6RF

JM/AC
Messrs Hall & Goode
21 Porter Street
Hull HU1 2RG   1 May 19..

Dear Sirs

We enclose order No 496 for electric lamps
and fittings, and shall be pleased to have
these by 15 May.

As we have not dealt with you previously,
we refer you to Messrs Smail & Sons,
42 Ryse Street, Chester CH4 8HJ who will
supply you with any necessary information.

Yours faithfully
for Thomas & Co
James Morton
(Manager)

MESSRS HALL & GOODE
21 Porter Street Hull HU1 2RG

PD/IH/29
Messrs Smail & Son   3rd May 19..
42 Ryse Street
Chester CH4 8HT

Dear Sirs

   We have received an opening order from Messrs Thomas & Co of 1 Greenbank Lane, Blackpool, FY1 6RF and they have referred us to you.

   We should be grateful to know whether you have had a long connection with this firm, and whether their transactions with you have always been settled promptly. Do they order freely? Would you consider it safe to allow them credit up to £200?

   Any information you supply will be treated in strict confidence. An early reply would be appreciated.

                    Yours faithfully
                    for Messrs Hall & Goode
                    Peter Duffy

In his reply the referee should answer carefully all the questions put to him, but he should avoid giving a definite guarantee of the integrity of the firm being discussed. It is advisable to avoid such phrases as—"You can safely give them credit up to £200." This may constitute bad advice. It is better to say—"We should not hesitate to give them credit up to £200."

Very often the name of the firm about which information is being given is omitted from the wording of the letter This is done to avoid possible complications should the letter fall into the possession of any unauthorized person. In such a case we use phrases as—"the firm you name" or "the firm whose name we enclose." The name of the firm is typed on a separate slip of paper and enclosed with the letter.

On the page opposite there is an example of a favourable reply to a status inquiry. On page 92 the example is of an unfavourable reply about credit.

				MESSRS SMAIL & SON
					42 Ryse Street
					Chester CH4 8HJ

5 May 19..

Messrs Hall & Goode
21 Porter Street
Hull
HU1 2RG

Dear Sirs

Thank you for your letter of 3 May, asking for information about the firm whose name we enclose.

This firm has been one of our regular customers for the past five years, sending us orders every three months. Payment has always been made on the due date and all transactions have been satisfactory.

We should be willing to allow credit up to £200; we have in fact had several orders from this firm for much larger amounts.

Yours faithfully
for Messrs Smail & Son
Edward Venner

EV/PH
enc

MESSRS SMAIL & SON
42 Ryse Street
Chester CH4 8HJ

5 May 19..

Messrs Hall & Goode
21 Porter Street
Hull
HU1 2RG

Dear Sirs

Thank you for your letter of 3 May, asking for information about the firm whose name we enclose.

We can only say, in reply, that our transactions with this firm have been so small that they do not justify an opinion from us about their financial standing.

We are sorry that we cannot give you any positive information that might encourage you to do business with them.

Yours faithfully
for Messrs Smail & Son
Edward Venner

EV/PH
enc

EXERCISE VI

Prepare letters from the following information—

1. (a) Beech & Heggie, 2 Cedar Road, Wolverhampton WV3 5TY send an order for goods value £100 to White & Co, 84 Runcorn Avenue, Leicester LE3 6FD. They name Farrell & Sons, Daimler Place, Leeds LS17 0ED as a reference.
   (b) White & Co, write to Farrell & Sons, asking for the necessary information about the Wolverhampton firm.
   (c) Farrell & Sons reply favourably.
   (d) Farrell & Sons reply unfavourably.
2. (a) Mills & Co, 4 Grey Lane, Berwick, ask Stevenson Bros, 69 Hull Road, York Y01 4GR, for information about Trainer & Gladstone, 24 Blacket Avenue, Newcastle NE5 3NT, who have sent them an order for £75 worth of gardening tools.
   (b) Stevenson Bros reply that they have had very few transactions with Trainer & Gladstone, but that, to the best of their knowledge, the latter firm is reputed to be reliable.
3. (a) A status inquiry is sent by a Liverpool firm to a Bradford firm, concerning Harmsworth & Son, 70 Barclay Street, Bolton BL1 2AX. Credit of £250 is asked for.
   (b) The Bradford firm reply that difficulty has been experienced in obtaining payment of accounts and they suggest that a smaller credit would be advisable.

LETTERS OF REFERENCE

These are in fact another form of status inquiry, seeking information on a specific point. On the following page there is an example of a letter asking for a foreign correspondent's reference.

James Roberts & Co. Ltd.
14 Prince Road Wolverhampton WV1 1HQ

AJ/MM
The Manager
Messrs Brown & Co Ltd
41 High Street
Sheffield S1 2GA

20 January 19..

Dear Sir

Miss Jane Ayton, who has applied to us for a post as Foreign Correspondent, has referred us to you for information about her ability, etc.

We shall be grateful therefore if you will say whether you consider her capable of taking the sole responsibility of a correspondence somewhat varied in character and whether her translation of English notes into German and French is both clear and accurate.

She speaks both languages fairly fluently, but naturally we wish to know whether she can also be relied upon to produce an exact translation of the English dictated to her.

We should appreciate hearing from you on the above points.

Yours faithfully
James Roberts & Co Ltd
Arthur Jamieson
(Secretary)

Here is the reply—

Brown & Co Ltd

41 High Street
Sheffield S1 2GA

JR/OF
The Secretary
James Roberts & Co Ltd
14 Prince Road
Wolverhampton WV1 1HQ

23rd January 19..

Dear Sir,

We have your letter of 20th January, enquiring about Miss Jane Ayton.

We are pleased to say that we consider her a first-class linguist. Miss Ayton has been with us for almost six years, and during the last two she has been in charge of all French and German correspondence. She is equally at home in both languages.

Miss Ayton is painstaking and always thorough in her work, and may be relied on to write business-like and exactly expressed letters. Her translation work is of a high order.

Miss Ayton has a pleasing and attractive personality, and we have found her character beyond reproach.

Your faithfully
Brown & Co Ltd
John Rimmer
(Manager)

Here is another example of a Letter of Reference—

T C Jepson & Co Ltd

4 Castle Street Dundee DD1 3AA

JS/RT/R
The Secretary
Chamber of Commerce
19 George Street
Edinburgh EH2 2PA   20 June 19..

Dear Sir

Miss Daphne Laker of 14 Abercrombie Place, Edinburgh has said that we might refer to you in respect of her application for the post of confidential secretary to one of our Directors.

Much of this Director's work is concerned with contracts and agreements, and this demands complete integrity, not to mention working under pressure from time to time. A considerable degree of initiative is also called for.

Your view on Miss Laker in these respects would be much appreciated, and will of course be treated in confidence. Perhaps you may prefer to telephone me.

Yours faithfully
T C Jepson & Co Ltd
John Shade
(Secretary)

And the reply—

THE CHAMBER OF COMMERCE
19 George Street Edinburgh EH2 2PA

DM/PW
The Secretary
T C Jepson & Co Ltd
4 Castle Street
Dundee DD1 3AA   23 June 19..

Dear Sir

Miss Daphne Laker

I have your inquiry about Miss Laker. This young lady has been with the Chamber, on the secretarial side, for four years. During this time she has always done good work, showing initiative and the ability to plan ahead. Her documentation work is accurate, her letters well-expressed, and she does not fluster under pressure.

Latterly Miss Laker has been handling some of the Chamber's confidential work; and I am certainly able to vouch for her integrity.

I am pleased to speak for Miss Laker.

                Yours faithfully
                  David Mann
                  (Secretary)

N.B. the reply above has been given a subject-heading; this is very often the practice in Letters of Reference.

LETTERS OF INTRODUCTION

A Letter of Introduction is what it says—a letter to introduce the representative of a firm to business houses in towns or districts to be visited. In such a letter we state his name, his connection with the firm, and his reason for travelling or visiting; we also request for him the advice and help of the firm addressed. We may mention our willingness to reciprocate should the opportunity arise.

N.B. a letter of introduction is not sealed unless, of course, it is sent through the post.

Study carefully the letter of introduction given on the page opposite.

Peel & Rose Ltd

5 Ryder Street
London EC2

Ref: JB/SM/105
Messrs Frank Ezar & Sons
381 Forty-Seventh Street
New York NY 10028   15 January 19..

Dear Sirs

This will introduce Mr Ronald Blair, the Head buyer for the Silks and Linen Department of our firm. Mr Blair is spending two months in the Eastern States in order to extend our business relations with American firms and to obtain new fabrics for possible introduction into the home market.

We shall be very grateful if you will introduce Mr Blair to reliable firms in the same line of business and if you will give him any personal assistance that may be necessary.

Your co-operation would be much appreciated.

Yours truly
For Peel & Rose Ltd
John Black
(Director)

EXERCISE VII

1. You have received a letter of application from Jonathan Dobson for the post of a cashier-bookkeeper in your firm. He has given you the name of his former employers.
   (a) Write to them for a reference.
   (b) As his former employer, reply favourably.

2. Miss Christine Troup has been supervisor of the typing pool in your firm (a large Assurance Company) for six months. She is moving to another town where she has applied for a similar post. The firm in question ask you for information about her ability and character.

   Write (a) a favourable reply and (b) a reply, favourable in respect of ability, but pointing out a defect in Miss Troup's character.

3. Write a letter of introduction to a Paris firm for your junior partner, Mr. Brian Foster, who is to be in France for a month to establish relations with French firms.

4. Write a letter to a firm notifying them of a visit by your representative.

CIRCULAR LETTERS

The purpose of a Circular Letter is to give information, e.g., change of address, extension of premises, introduction of new lines, opening of a new branch, etc. The essence of a circular letter therefore must be accuracy and clarity.

It should be brief. If it is long, it will probably not be read; if it is short, it will in most cases at least be read. It is essential therefore to word the circular in such a way that the reader's attention is held from the beginning.

The following points should be included in a letter announcing the opening of a new branch—

(a) *where*, *when* and *why* the branch will be opened.
(b) a description, attractively worded, of the stock offered.
(c) an invitation to visit the new premises.

Here is an example of this type of circular letter.

> ### *Norse & Co*
> 14 George Street
> Edinburgh EH2 9JZ
> 15th October 19..
>
> Dear Sir/Madam,
>
> We have pleasure in informing you that, because of the increased demand for our sportswear in the West of Scotland, we are opening a new branch of our business on 1st November at—
>
> 40 Renfield Street
> Glasgow C2
>
> We shall have on display at our new branch a most attractive collection of Ski-ing Outfits which have just arrived from Norway. The designs are original, the colourings gay, and the prices, we feel, are moderate.
>
> May we suggest an early visit to our showrooms in Renfield Street? Our manager (Mr. Arthur Black) or one of his assistants will be pleased to welcome you and show you round.
>
> Yours faithfully
> NORSE & CO

EXERCISE VIII

1. A firm of fountain-pen manufacturers has produced a new type of pen. Write a circular letter to be sent by the firm to dealers.
2. King & Blaikie, Ladies' Outfitters, 8–10 Ford Place, Cardiff CF5 4NR have just made a large extension of premises. This extension, to be opened in two weeks' time, contains several new departments, an up-to-date restaurant and lounge.

    Write a circular from King & Blaikie to their customers, stressing the advantages of this venture.
3. Pierce & Hogg, 8 Mornington Street, Derby DE3 4BB, send a circular to customers to announce their summer sale of footwear and hosiery, and enclose illustrated literature.

    Write their circular letter.

EXERCISE IX

Write the following Circular Letters—

1. From a newly-opened greengrocer's shop to prospective customers in the district.
2. From a carpet firm to its customers, intimating an extension of premises.
3. From the Gas Board in your local area, giving details of a new gas-cooker and offering generous trade-in terms for old cookers.
4. From a sports outfitter, at the approach of the cricket season, to secretaries of local clubs, offering special terms of discount on purchases by clubs.
5. From a wine merchant, to his customers, intimating the closure of his premises because of building redevelopment, and his removal to new premises in one of the city suburbs.

LETTERS OF APPLICATION

It is essential to remember that a Letter of Application is normally your first introduction to a prospective employer. Therefore your letter must be clear and concise, correct and courteous. A letter badly written creates a poor impression; on the other hand, a neat and coherent letter, its facts well put together, is certain to make a favourable impression.

Therefore, keep your letter free from errors, punctuate it correctly, paragraph it sensibly. It should of course be handwritten—unless a typewritten reply to the advertisement has been specially asked for, and this is unlikely.

Remembering again the importance of first impressions, plan and arrange your letter carefully, You must include certain essential facts; these are—

(a) formal application
(b) reference to the advertisement
(c) age and education
(d) commercial/secretarial training, with a note of standards reached or examinations passed
(e) any previous employment or experience
(f) your willingness to attend for interview

There are, however, other points to remember about a letter of application

It is normal practice to make reference to a referee, giving name and address where necessary. You must, of course, obtain permission before quoting a referee.

Should testimonials be asked for, send typed copies, *not* the originals.

It may be politic to state the reason for leaving your present post. If so, do not hesitate to give the reason but state it simply and clearly.

Finally, and this is very important; take careful note of the information required by the advertisement. In your reply, overlook nothing that has been asked for.

On the two following pages there are some examples of letters of application. Both are for first posts—

(a) a junior shorthand-typist, (b) a secretary

4 Radner Lane
Glasgow C.3.
17th April, 19..

Messrs. Hurst and Barron,
53 Wellington Street,
Glasgow, C.1.

Dear Sirs,
  I wish to apply for the post of Junior Shorthand-Typist as advertised in the "Herald" of 16th April.

  I shall be 17 years of age next month. I was educated at Poston High School and left at the end of my fourth year with three "O" level passes in English, Arithmetic and Homecraft.

  I have just completed a year's course at Stead's Secretarial College in Glasgow taking examinations in Shorthand, Typing, Elementary Accounts, Business English and Business Procedure. I have gained certificates in Shorthand at 80 w.a.m (R.S.A.); Typing at 40 w.a.m. (R.S.A.); Elementary Accounts; Business English and Business Procedure.

  The Principal of Stead's College, Mr. W.F. Morton, M.A. has given me permission to name him as a referee.

  I am available for interview at any time.

       Yours faithfully,
       Jane Cummings

17 March Lane,
Stafford.
5th September, 19..

Dear Sir,

I wish to apply for the post of Secretary as advertised in yesterday's "Evening Post".

I am nineteen and a half years of age and was educated at St Hilda's Girls' School where I gained five "O" level passes and one "A" level pass in French.

On leaving school I took the Higher Secretarial Course at Middlehurst Ladies' College. This is the College's senior course and covers Shorthand, Typewriting, Accounts, Secretarial Duties, Correspondence and Communications, and Commercial French.

I have R.S.A. passes in Shorthand (120 w.a.m.), Typewriting (Advanced), and Secretarial Duties (Stage II). In addition, I speak reasonably fluent French and have a good working knowledge of French business correspondence.

The following people have agreed to act as referees on my behalf: B. Johnson, Esq., B.A, F.R.S.A. Principal, Middlehurst Ladies College, Middlehurst, Kent and J.R. Martin, Esq. Q.C. The Wynd, Blackburn, near Stafford.

I am available for interview at any time.

Yours faithfully,
Doreen L. James

Box No. 144,
Evening Post, Stafford.

N.B. In (*a*) and (*b*) on pp. 104 and 105, the relevant information is given in the body of the letter.

Remember also, that as you have no actual working experience, it is important to emphasize your training, particularly the examinations you have passed.

Later, as you gain in working experience and move on from your first post, it may be preferable to give the details of your qualifications, etc., in an enclosure (typed by yourself) and not in the body of the letter. With this enclosure you should send a handwritten covering letter.

An example of such a letter is given on the facing page. Notice that it is in reply to a Box number advertisement. There is an example of the schedule which should accompany it on page 108.

Exercises for practice are to be found on pages 109–114.

5, Queen's Gate,
Durham,
6th May, 19..

The Advertiser,
Box 115, "Durham News",
Durham.

Dear Sir,
   I wish to apply for the post of Private Secretary advertised in the "Durham News" on 4th May.
   The enclosed schedule gives details of my qualifications and experience.
   My present firm, Messrs. Small and Peacock of 12 Bread Lane, Durham, are in the process of being taken over and, as a result, a secretarial pool is being introduced. My preference has always been to work for one or two executives. This, I feel, allows scope for one's own initiative. Therefore I am now seeking a similar type of post to that which I have held for the last four years.
   You may, of course, refer to my present employer who knows why I am looking for another post.
   I am available for interview by arrangement.

                           Yours faithfully,
                           Sheena Robson

Enc.

SCHEDULE OF DETAILS

Name	Sheena Barclay Robson
Age	25 years (date of birth : 19.10.19 . .)
Education	Calder Girls School, Cumberland, 19 . . to 19 . . G.C.E.: 7 "O" levels 2 "A"levels (English and French) Newcastle College of Education, one year's secretarial course, 19 . . to 19 . . Shorthand: RSA Certificate, 140 wpm Typewriting: RSA Certificate, Stage III (Advanced) Present speed : 70 wpm Other certificates taken in college course: Secretarial Practice. Correspondence and Communications, Principles of Accounts, Commercial French.
Experience	Oct 19 . . to Aug 19 . . (2 years) Assistant Secretary, Educational Section, Carver's Publications Ltd, Newcastle upon Tyne, NE2 5TS. Sept 19 . . to date (4 years) Private Secretary to Sales Director, Small & Peacock, 12 Bread Lane, Derby DE2 5LY. Present Duties: Private Secretarial work, conference arrangements, report and statistical work, confidential documentation, translation work (French).
Referees	Robert P. Jackson Q.C., The Mill House, Green Lane, Gosforth, Newcastle upon Tyne NET 5TS. Mr. D.A. Illingworth, Sales Director, Messrs Small and Peacock, 12 Bread Lane, Derby DE2 5LY.

EXERCISE X

Write letters of application in reply to the following advertisements:

1. *Wanted:* Junior for office work. Previous experience not essential. Good typing speed. Apply, with full particulars, to Box JS 415 "Evening News."

2. *Shorthand-typist* required by busy advertising agency; experience in this field desirable but not essential; must be competent in speed and accuracy; good telephone manner. Apply in writing to Hall Advertising Ltd., 110 Wellington Place, Glasgow C2.

3. *Shorthand/audio typist* required for secretarial duties, including preparation of agenda and minutes, in central administrative office. Good salary scale. 38-hour week. Work is interesting and there are promotion prospects. Write Personnel Officer, Royal Infirmary, Leeds LS2 9LR quoting Ref RIL/SA.

4. *Receptionist/typist* wanted by British Typewriters Ltd. Typing, switchboard, receiving visitors and conducting showroom sales. Applicants (age about 20) must be first-class typists, have a smart appearance, cheerful personality and a pleasant voice. Salary attractive for right applicant, plus luncheon vouchers, plus commission on sales. There is plenty of work to do, no time for knitting. The successful applicant must be polite and efficient always, even when harassed. Write Mr J. Matthews at 151 West Nile Street, Glasgow C2.

5. *Shorthand-typist* required by large electrical wholesaler. Efficient speeds in shorthand and typing essential. Knowledge of German a recommendation. Good conditions. Canteen facilities. Full particulars to Box 9168 "Daily Post," Hull HU2 3DE.

6. **Wanted for an American Company**
   SECRETARY
   to the Personnel Manager.

   Work in modern conditions and with the latest equipment. Dealing with people rather than things. You will be well paid and your work will be important. Five-day week, subsidised canteen, non-contributing pension scheme.

Write or phone
Mr John Bowman
Personnel Manager

THE SHAPER CO LTD
Pond Place, West Close, Bath BA2 1PY
Tel: West Kilbride 20451

7. SOUTH-WESTERN HOSPITAL BOARD, SCOTLAND
   Treasurer's Department
   Personal Assistant

   Applications are invited for the post of Personal Assistant to the Treasurer. Good speeds in shorthand and typing and ability to prepare financial and statistical statements essential. The successful candidate will be responsible for the day to day running of the Secretarial Section of the Treasurer's Department. Post carries superannuation. Five-day week. Canteen facilities. Applications in writing with full particulars to be sent to—

   Secretary, South-Western Hospital Board, Scotland, 11 Drumsheugh Gardens, Edinburgh EH3 7QG.

8. *Typing & clerical assistant* required for architect's office. Experience not essential but competency a must. Salary by arrangement. Tom Cook Associates, Lumley Street, Grangemouth.

9. *Audio-typist* wanted by incorporated insurance brokers. Applicant must have sound training/experience, with ability to write reports. Pleasant working conditions. Application in writing to—Staff Manager, Stillhouse Ltd., 10 York Place, Nottingham NG5 4PU.

10.
> # Secretary-Typists
>
> Applications invited for following posts in—
>
> Student Accommodation
> Natural Philosophy
> Veterinary School
> Computer Department
>
> Good standard of education and
> secretarial qualifications necessary
>
> Generous holidays
>
> Superannuation Scheme
>
> Apply in writing to the Secretary,
> University of Nottingham, NG7 2RD
> specifying post applied for.

TELEGRAMS

Telegrams are normally used only in emergency. It is important therefore that their language should be clear and concise, but in no circumstances should clarity of understanding be waived for brevity.

In a telegram all unnecessary words are omitted. The salutation and complimentary ending are dispensed with; only the essentials for understanding are stated, in as brief a form as possible.

N.B. A telegram is typed in capitals.

EXERCISE XI

Prepare telegrams for the following—

1. To the Manager, Seaview Hotel, Blackpool FY1 5LE, to reserve a single room for three nights for Mr Edward Horton, Bellevue Hotel, Manchester M10 9EP. Specify dates.

2. To Messrs Hope & Parry, County House, Main Street, Plymouth PL3 4LW, postponing Mr Paterson's visit for a few days. Give a reason for the postponement.
3. To Cooper Ltd, Hoxton Mills, Sale, Cheshire M33 2HX, increasing the order of the previous day to 50 doz. white towels.
4. To a firm who have not fulfilled an order of goods by the specified date. Immediate delivery is now urgent. Supply names, etc.

EXERCISE XII

1. You have received a letter from the Unity Assurance Company intimating that their representative proposes to call to discuss a Staff Pensions Assurance Scheme. Reply—
   (a) politely that your staff are already insured for superannuation and that no useful purpose would be served by the proposed visit.
   (b) with reference to the proposed visit, that you will be too busy to consider the matter until after the end of the month, and suggest a date early in the following month.
2. Your firm (an estate agency) is opening a small branch office Write to a bookseller ordering a small stock of reference books.
3. Prepare a letter to Hardwell & Croft, Deansgate, Manchester, asking them to quote prices for curtains for 60 bedroom windows at the New Clarendon Hotel, Edinburgh EH5 5BW. The dimensions of the windows are 8 ft by 3 ft 9 in. Ask for recommendations of materials that will be durable and washable. Patterns to be sent with quotations.
4. As secretary of a large commercial organization in London, write to the Head Office of a Trust Hotels chain asking for special terms on arrangements for your travelling representatives. Stress the high frequency of their travel.

   Also, write the reply from Head Office to the secretary.
5. Your firm are wholesale box-makers. Write to one of your retailers, apologizing for both wrong delivery of goods ordered

and for late delivery. Arrange for immediate replacement by special delivery.

6. The Scott Laundry Co, Hove BN3 1GF have had the contract for laundering the linen of the Lion Hotel, Hove BN3 4QY for three years. Lately the quality of the work done has deteriorated.

    (a) Send a suitable letter pointing this out and asking that the matter be investigated.

    (b) Reply from the Scott Laundry Co, apologizing for the defects reported by the Lion Hotel. Promise to investigate the cause of the inferior work. One possible explanation is the introduction of some new hands in the package and delivery section.

7. Write a circular letter from the Pembroke Water Board to householders in a local area, giving notice of a temporary loss of water supply. Give the reason and specify times and details. Also, draft a notice of the above facts for insertion in the local press.

8. (a) Send an inquiry to Messrs Finsbury & Sons, Milton Street, Bath BA1 1LG asking why their representative has not made his usual half-yearly call on your firm (I. & G. Holly, Gloucester Green, Cambridge CB3 8NL.) You are running short of stock and are anxious to see samples of Finsbury's productions for the summer season. Specify items in which you are particularly interested.

    (b) Write a reply to I. & G. Holly, Gloucester Green, Cambridge CB3 8NL from Finsbury & Sons. Mr Hodgson, their former representative, left the firm very recently, and his successor, Mr John Bray, has taken rather longer to make his round of their area, but is expected to be in Cambridge at the end of the month. He will have with him some new samples of items which can be dispatched at once from stock.

9. You have ordered and had delivered to your home a suitcase which you are giving to someone as a present. The initials on the case have been wrongly engraved. There is, in addition, a

slight dent in one corner. You are a good account customer of the shop. Write, giving details, etc.

(*a*) your letter of complaint
(*b*) the reply from the manager of the shop

–10–

The Art of Précis

WHAT IS A PRÉCIS? A précis is a summary, in narrative form, of the subject-matter of a report, letter, series of letters, or any other kind of document or series of documents. Although it is a summary, a précis must be written in good English and not in the abbreviated English of telegrams.

WHAT IS THE PURPOSE OF A PRÉCIS? Your boss may wish to know all the important facts of a certain matter about which there has been considerable correspondence over a long period. He has not the time to read all the letters many of which may not contain important facts. He therefore instructs you to write out in narrative form a précis which must contain all the main points of the matter. All unimportant details should be omitted. When completed the précis should give all essential and relevant features of the matter under examination so that no reference need be made to the correspondence.

HOW BRIEF SHOULD A PRÉCIS BE? This is not always easy to determine, but it should be as brief as the inclusion of all important matters will permit. Normally, one-third of the number of words in the original matter is sufficient to achieve this.

All direct speech in the original matter must be turned into indirect speech in the précis. For example—

> The Chairman said, "The situation is one of great difficulty, and we may be forced to ease our attitude to shift-work."

If the whole of this statement is to be included in a précis, it should appear as follows—

The Chairman said that the situation was one of great difficulty, and they might be forced to ease their attitude to shift-work.

N.B. A précis should be written in the past tense and in the third person.

Characteristics of a good précis

These are as follows—

LOGICAL ORDER. The facts should be set out in their proper order and sequence.

COMPLETENESS. The précis must contain sufficient details to enable the subject to be understood in all its aspects without reference to the original.

GOOD ENGLISH. The rules of grammar must be obeyed. Slang expressions and abbreviations as in a telegram should not appear in a précis.

CONTINUITY. The sentences should read easily and smoothly.

PRECISENESS. Care must be taken to express the exact meaning of the original, even although the matter is condensed and summarized.

When making a précis, try to follow these stages—

(*a*) Read through the original, if possible twice, grasp the topic dealt with and gain a clear idea of the subject-matter.

(*b*) Make an outline of the précis before writing it.

(*c*) Make a rough draft and compare it with the original; be sure you have included everything of importance and excluded all unimportant detail.

(*d*) Write the précis.

The précis must be a summary of the whole of the original and not several small summaries of parts of the original. Do not therefore make the mistake of writing summaries of the parts of the original and then putting them all together as one. For instance, if the circumstances of a matter are contained in a dozen letters written over a period of time, you should not make a summary of each letter. You must grasp the main topic of them all as a whole

THE ART OF PRÉCIS

and then, in a narrative form, make your summary on this topic, taking all the important details from each letter.

N.B. Economy of words is essential. Here are two examples.

(a) Replying to the statement of the chairman, Mr Smith said he did not accept that view of the matter.

This can be shortened to—

Mr Smith disagreed with the chairman's view.

(b) It seems to me that your company or your directors or your manager have shown little consideration for the special requirements of the firms for whom I am speaking. We are entitled therefore to ask that these requirements shall be more fully met in future; if not these firms will not unnaturally seek their supplies elsewhere.

This can be shortened to—

Expressing dissatisfaction with the attitude of the Company, the speaker urged that his clients' requests should have due attention if their dealings were to be continued.

Your boss may ask you to write a short summary or précis of a series of correspondence similar to that which appears below. Could you do it? For practice, write a précis of the series of letters that starts on the following page. Then compare your version with the précis given on page 120.

1.

James Russell & Co.

14 WALKER STREET
EDINBURGH EH1 2AY

Messrs Henry Kay & Co
97 Park Road
Derby DE3 4HX   17th March 19..

Dear Sirs,

  We have pleasure in enclosing confirmation of our order for next season's goods. Will you please give this matter your attention and deliver the order as soon as possible?

                 Yours faithfully,
Encl   James Russell & Co

2.

HENRY KAY & CO

                               97 Park Road
                               Derby
                               DE3 4HX

Messrs James Russell & Co
14 Walker Street
Edinburgh EH1 2AY   19 March 19..

Dear Sirs

Thank you for your order for next season's goods. We have put this in hand, and shall do our best to deliver them without delay.

Yours faithfully
Henry Kay & Co

James Russell & Co.

14 WALKER STREET
EDINBURGH EH1 2AY

Messrs Henry Kay & Co
97 Park Road
Derby DE3 4HX

15th April 19..

Dear Sirs,

  Our customer threatens to cancel the goods on order if they are not delivered immediately. Can you do anything to help us in this matter by anticipating the date of delivery?

                          Yours faithfully,
                          James Russell & Co

HENRY KAY & CO

97 Park Road
Derby
DE3 4HX
18 April 19..

Messrs James Russell & Co
14 Walker Street
Edinburgh EH1 2AY

Dear Sirs

  In reply to your letter of 15 April, we wish to say that we are doing our utmost to complete your order. We hope to send the goods by the end of the present week. We have not lost any available time, and trust that the goods will be in time for your client.

Yours faithfully
Henry Kay & Co

James Russell & Co.

14 WALKER STREET
EDINBURGH EH1 2AY

20th April 19..

Messrs Henry Kay & Co
97 Park Road
Derby DE3 4HX

Dear Sirs,

  We are glad to receive your assurance this morning that the goods will be delivered by the end of the present week.

  Our customer positively refuses to wait beyond that time.

                    Yours faithfully,
                    James Russell & Co

Here is the précis that you might have written.

Précis of Correspondence Between Messrs James Russell & Co, 14 Walker Street, Edinburgh EH1 2AY and Messrs Henry Kay & Co, 97 Park Road, Derby DE3 4HX, Dated 17th March to 20th April 19 . .

On 17th March 19 . . Messrs James Russell & Co Edinburgh, placed an order for next season's goods with Messrs Henry Kay & Co, Derby, who promised that every endeavour would be made to meet the request for early delivery. However, as Messrs Russell & Co had not received the goods by 15th April, they informed Messrs Kay & Co that their customer now insisted on immediate delivery, otherwise he would cancel the order. They were assured that everything was being done to arrange delivery by the end of the week at the latest.

  Similarly, you may be asked to write a précis of a speech. Here, to help you, is an example of a speech followed by a précis of it.

THE ART OF PRÉCIS

A Company Chairman's Speech

At Frome, with a crop of 68,250 tons, we surpassed all previous records. This is indeed a testimony to the whole organization at Frome, to the field staff for having maintained high deliveries of cane to the mill, and to the factory staff for maintaining such high efficiency throughout a long crop.

At Monymusk we started crop with the old factory, which continued to operate until the completion of our large new factory. In my statement last year I anticipated that the new factory would be completed by about the end of March. In fact, a start was made on the 6th of April, and, having regard to all the difficulties attending such large scale construction in these difficult times, I feel that the effort reflects great credit upon our engineers and construction personnel, who achieved completion more or less in accordance with schedule. As with all new factories, experience over several crops will be needed in order to achieve the maximum standard of efficiency.

As indicative of the developments for which our company has been responsible, I would mention that twelve years ago on the areas now owned by us some 45,000 tons of sugar were produced in nine old factories. In the crop now commenced we hope to produce over 120,000 tons of sugar in two modern factories. I can assure you that we are keeping abreast of technical developments and that we are deriving great value from the various research units we have established.

But, however interesting facts and figures bearing upon the material progress made by our company may be, we must never lose sight of the fact that a proper understanding of human problems is basic to all our endeavours. We are aiming to knit together in our undertaking a team which can function in a happy unity and to the maximum benefit of all concerned. This is an ideal for which we shall always strive, guided by those on the spot with first-hand knowledge of the problems involved. It is not a subject which lends itself to theorizing, nor indeed to modelling on patterns in other countries where different circumstances may exist.

(360 words)

Précis of Company Chairman's Speech

The Chairman reported that the increased output at Frome was a testimony to the efficiency of the whole organization. The completion of the new factory at Monymusk almost on the expected date was a matter for congratulation of the constructional staff. The full standard of efficiency should be reached in the coming years.

Whereas, previously, the production of sugar from nine old factories had been 45,000 tons, the two new factories should produce 120,000 tons. Success however depended upon the human element, and the ideal at which the Company would continue to aim was a spirit of unity and common purpose throughout the staff.

In this they would rely not on what happened in other countries, but on the experience and advice of those who had first-hand knowledge of all conditions in this country.

(140 words)

Précis (Recapitulation)

Requirements of a good Précis

1. Your summary must contain all important facts and must omit all unimportant details.
2. Its length should not be more than one-third of the original— or as required.
3. Speeches and articles in direct speech must be changed to indirect speech.
4. Language and style must be simple and clear.
5. Points made must be in logical sequence; and connection of ideas should be kept clear.
6. Your précis must be written in the past tense.

The Method to be followed

1. Read the passage; make sure that you know what it is all about.
2. Find a title, indicating in it the main topic.

3. Read the passage again, slowly. Underline essential points which must be included in the finished précis.
4. Make brief notes of these points in your own words.
5. Put aside the original passage; make a continuous summary from your own notes only.
6. Count the words in this summary; adjust, if necessary.
7. Compare with the original.
8. Write out a fair copy of your précis.
9. Check that it is in good, readable English and that both grammar and punctuation are correct.
10. Include at the end the number of words (less those in the title).

EXERCISE I

Wool Prices

Once again it is advisable to appreciate that the monetary turnover is, to a large extent, governed by the price level of wool; but your directors have much pleasure in advising that during the year a substantial increase has occurred in the number of clients who are regularly purchasing part of their requirements through this company. According to all available information, wool must still be regarded as statistically very sound, but one is forced to the conclusion that there is an increasing resistance on the part of consumers to the very high prices now prevailing. This may result in an increasing use of substitutes, thus slowing up the demand for wool from the consuming centres of the world.

1. Summarize the above extract.
2. What word would you substitute for "appreciate" in the first line?
3. What is meant by the statement that "wool is statistically sound"?
4. Simplify the statement—"there is an increasing resistance on the part of customers to the very high prices now prevailing."

ENGLISH FOR BUSINESS

EXERCISE II

Make a précis of the following correspondence—

1.

Sadler & Co.
14 Argyle Street Glasgow C2

Sharp & Co Ltd
35 North Street
Leeds LS6 8HT   6 May 19..

Dear Sirs

Thank you for your furniture catalogue received today. We note that you have introduced a number of new lines, and shall send you orders for these later. In the meantime, please forward to us:

3 Jacobean Dining-room Suites No 197
4 Kitchen Cabinets No 35

As business is brisk at present, we should like to have these goods by 13 May.

Yours faithfully
pp Sadler & Co
William Wright

2.

Sharp & Co., Ltd.   35 North Street Leeds LS6 8HT

Messrs Sadler & Co
14 Argyle Street
Glasgow C2   8 May 19..

Dear Sirs

We thank you for your order of 6 May
for:
    3 Jacobean Dining-room Suites No 197
    4 Kitchen Cabinets No 35

We are forwarding these goods to you by
van tomorrow.

Yours faithfully
pp Sharp & Co Ltd
C. Upton

Sadler & Co.
14 Argyle Street Glasgow C2

```
Sharp & Co Ltd
35 North Street
Leeds LS6 8HT                 11 May 19..
```

Dear Sirs

The furniture ordered by us on 6 May was delivered this morning and we thank you for your prompt attention to our order.

We regret to state, however, that the glass in one of the kitchen cabinets is cracked, and that the lock is faulty. We shall be glad if you will send for the cabinet and repair it, or replace it.

Yours faithfully,
pp Sadler & Co
William Wright

Sharp & Co., Ltd.   35 North Street Leeds LS6 8HT

Messrs Sadler & Co
14 Argyle Street
Glasgow C2   13 May 19.

Dear Sirs

We very much regret to note from your
letter of 11 May that one of the kitchen
cabinets delivered to you was faulty.

Our van is to be in Glasgow at the end of
this week and we shall arrange to deliver
a kitchen cabinet to replace the damaged
one which our vanman will collect from
you.

We trust that you will have no cause for
further complaint, and that we shall have
the pleasure of receiving further orders
from you.

Yours faithfully
pp Sharp & Co Ltd
C. Upton

EXERCISE III

Write a précis of the following article (*360 words*), reducing it to 120 words. Give it a title.

Plans for the first really major development in the weaving section of textiles for more than half a century were revealed here today by Cassels.

The group is to spend £2,500,000 on a new factory at Carlisle to be equipped with machinery giving three to four times the output of a conventional weaving mill. Three other new weaving factories, all on a smaller scale, are planned by Cassels and details of these are to be announced later this year. They will all be in the north of England.

The new Carlisle plant, in which high speed 130 in. wide looms are to be installed, will employ 250 people—most of them men—whom Cassels will recruit and train locally.

The choice of Carlisle for the factory, rather than one of the Lancashire cotton towns, is interesting. Carlisle has a longstanding association with textiles, but its main virtue from Cassels' point of view is that it lies within a development area, and the project will, therefore, qualify for investment grants.

The other important consideration is that in order to operate at maximum efficiency the plant will have to be run on a three-shift basis. There are therefore some advantages in taking it outside the traditional weaving areas where working practices are firmly established. Labour difficulties are unlikely, in any case, since the plans received an enthusiastic welcome from the textile union leaders.

Cassels will be anxious, during the period before the plant comes into operation early next year, to impress on their friends and customers among the established Lancashire weavers that it does not constitute a threat to them, or their future.

The Carlisle plant will be used almost exclusively for weaving heavier weight cloths, covering a whole range of blends and mixtures of spun yarn, incorporating both natural and man-made fibres, for the clothing trade.

Cassels also make the point that their new weaving plants will be closely integrated with their Northern Textiles Spinning Division, which has already announced a £12m. re-equipment programme which is said to be "proceeding according to schedule."

EXERCISE IV

Make a précis of the following correspondence—

1.

Orwell & Tainsh
5 Arden Road, Aberdeen AB5 0YN

Messrs Balfour & Sons
216 Leyton Road
Carlisle   12th October 19..

Dear Sirs,

The stationery we ordered from you on 7th October was delivered to us this afternoon by the Sendkwik Delivery Co.

We find, however, that some of the goods are missing, viz—

      10 quires "Crema" foolscap
      5 gross "Bestwrite"
      assorted lead pencils.

We trust you will look into the matter, and have these goods sent without delay.

                Yours faithfully
                pp Orwell & Tainsh
                Maxwell Finnie

Balfour & Sons

216 Leyton Road Carlisle

The Sendkwik Delivery Co
3-5 Juniper Lane
Dumfries   14 October 19..

Dear Sirs

On 12 October one of your vans took a
consignment of stationery from our
warehouse to Messrs Orwell & Tainsh, 5
Arden Road, Aberdeen AB5 0YN. We have
just received a letter from this firm,
complaining that

10 quires "Crema" foolscap, and
5 gross "Bestwrite" assorted lead pencils

have not been received. The order was
carefully checked before dispatch, and we
think these items must have gone astray in
transit.

Will you please make inquiries and forward
the goods at once to our customers?

                                        Yours faithfully
                                        pp Balfour & Sons
                                        David Thomas

3.

Benton & Co

41 Hanover Street
Perth

The Sendkwik Delivery Co
3-5 Juniper Lane
Dumfries   14 October 19..

Dear Sirs

On checking the consignment of stationery
delivered by your van on 12 October, we
find we have received ten quires of
foolscap and five gross of lead pencils in
excess of order. These were probably
intended for some other firm. The labels
are indecipherable.

We are returning these goods to you
today, carriage forward, by rail.

                                  Yours faithfully
                                  pp Benton & Co
                                  Ralph Younger

THE SENDKWIK DELIVERY CO
3–5 Juniper Lane, Dumfries

Messrs Balfour & Sons
216 Leyton Road
Carlisle
15 October 19..

Dear Sirs

We have your letter of yesterday notifying
us of the non-delivery to your customers,
Messrs Orwell & Tainsh, 5 Arden Road,
Aberdeen AB5 OYN of—

10 quires "Crema" foolscap, and
 5 gross "Bestwrite" assorted lead
   pencils.

We have just been informed by a firm in
Perth that these goods have been delivered
to them along with their own order. They
state that the labels are blurred and
torn, and that the parcels are being
returned to us.

We shall send these goods direct to Messrs
Orwell & Tainsh as soon as we receive
them, and trust you will overlook our
error.

Please accept our sincere apologies for
the inconvenience caused to your customer.

Yours truly
pp The Sendkwik Delivery Co
Arthur Hamilton
Manager

THE ART OF PRÉCIS

EXERCISE V

Write a précis of the following passage. Your précis should not exceed 120 words.

COMPUTER CONTROLS LIMITED

The 29th Annual General Meeting of Computer Controls Limited was held on November 3rd 19 . . in London, the Chairman Mr A. P. Harris presiding.

The following are extracts from his Statement circulated with the Report and Accounts for the year ended 31st March, 19 . ..

Accounts: The results for the trading year showed a profit of £585,751. The Directors recommend a Final Dividend of $3\frac{1}{2}$%, making a total of 20% for the year. Your Directors have consistently carried out a conservative policy in respect of the proportion of earnings to be distributed as dividends, since a part of the profits must be retained to provide the finance necessary for the expansion of the Company's business.

Exports: Exports amounted to 42% of the Group turnover and I believe that this figure is higher than the average for our branch of industry. By doing so we almost reached the target set by ourselves and to which reference was made in my statement of last year. The short fall was mostly due to the difficulties encountered in the countries which are members of the Common Market of Europe. All the same, I would like to record the export achievement of British Controls Corporation, the Company's biggest subsidiary, whose sales abroad amounted to practically 55% of their turnover.

Prospects: The order book fell 10% during the financial year under review. Since the end of the year, however, the trend has been reversed, and the figure to date is in advance of the figure 12 months ago.

At the present moment it is extremely difficult to attempt to forecast future trends of profits. The economic indications in the United Kingdom are far from promising, and the inflationary tendencies in costs and pressure on profit margins are likely to continue. Fortunately our Company has a high proportion of export business and a satisfactory order book, and we look to our present Management Team for improved results in the future.

The Report and Accounts were adopted and the other formal business duly transacted.

(340 words)

EXERCISE VI

Make a précis of the following correspondence—

1.

ANGUS WATSON & CO
Ellison House, Newcastle upon Tyne, NE1 6LH

Mr A.P.King
Paloma
Beverly Hills
California USA
17th March 19..

Dear Sir,

Our success in the sale of the consignment of fruit received from you last summer has suggested the possibility of developing a profitable business in tinned Californian fruit, principally pears, plums and peaches, and we should very much appreciate your considered opinion of this proposition.

We presume there are fruit canneries in your district, and, judging from the superior quality of the fresh fruit we have had from you, we think it should be quite possible to obtain a really good line in tinned fruits which would be readily saleable in England.

May we ask you, therefore, to go into
the matter for us; to give us definite
particulars of the supplies available; to
send sample tins, with prices, of each of
the fruits mentioned; and to tell us
whether the quality and canning can always
be relied upon?

If the guarantees and prices are
satisfactory, we feel we can promise very
considerable orders.

We shall, or course, ask you to deal
with the Californian firms on our behalf.

We look forward to having an early reply
from you. You will appreciate, we are
sure, that we are anxious to establish
this new development as soon as possible.

Yours faithfully
Angus Watson & Co

Paloma, Beverly Hills, California, USA

Messrs Angus Watson & Co
Ellison House
Newcastle upon Tyne NE1 6LH
31 March 19..

Dear Sirs

I thank you for your letter asking me to investigate the question of sending tinned fruits from California to England, and assure you that I welcome the prospect of doing further business with you.

The fruit canning industry is already well developed here, and I believe there is no better product anywhere. I have sent you a sample selection from two of the leading canneries, accompanied by a fully detailed schedule of prices and terms.

With regard to the proposed agency, I shall be pleased to act for you on a two per cent basis, and trust this arrangement will be acceptable to you. I shall be able to arrange for three months' credit and, subject to your approval, would draw upon you at ninety days to cover the cost, freight and my commission.

The prices which are quoted for quantities will, I think, attract you, and I am confident that the business will prove a remunerative one. You may certainly rely on the ability and determination of the canners to maintain the excellence of the goods.

I hope to be favoured with your orders.

Yours truly
A P King

ANGUS WATSON & CO.
Ellison House, Newcastle upon Tyne, NE1 6LH

Mr A.P.King
Paloma
Beverly Hills
California, USA
1st May 19..

Dear Sir,

The sample selection of tinned fruits advised in your letter of 31st March has arrived, and we consider it justifies your belief that it would meet with our approval. They are of excellent quality and are certain to command a ready market here if we can amend the prices slightly.

The selling prices, after allowing for all costs and a small margin of profit for ourselves, are just a little high to turn the scale in our favour with dealers who have been stocking other varieties, and we must ask you to do your best to lower the quotation by five per cent. If it will help you with the canners, you can state that we expect to be able to place orders for well over a thousand cases within the next six months.

If you are successful, please arrange to have the enclosed order for twenty gross assorted fruits executed and shipped as early as possible, notifying us by cable of the name of the vessel and date of sailing, so that we can arrange the insurance here.

To cover the value of the order, freight, and your commission of two per cent, you may draw upon us at ninety days and your draft will be duly honoured.

Yours faithfully
Angus Watson & Co

cable
> WATSON, ELLISON HOUSE, NEWCASTLE UPON TYNE NE1 6LH, ENGLAND. TWENTY GROSS ASSORTED FRUITS, 60 CASES, S.S. AJAX, SAILING FIRST JUNE.
>
> KING.

Paloma, Beverly Hills, California, USA

Messrs Angus Watson & Co
Ellison House
Newcastle upon Tyne NE1 6LH
England
28 May 19..

Dear Sirs

My cable to you dated 27 May announced the dispatch from San Francisco on 1 June, of twenty gross of Assorted Fruits packed in sixty cases per SS AJAX, via Panama.

From this you will have inferred that I secured the reduction in price which you stipulated and though the canners were very loth to reduce their earlier quotation I was able to convince them that the promised business was too good to lose. I hope to hear in due course that the shipment reaches you in time, and that the goods meet with immediate approval from dealers.

I have today drawn upon you, at ninety days, for the amount of my account, as shown in the enclosed statement.

Yours truly
A P King
Encl

THE ART OF PRÉCIS

EXERCISE VII

CHAIRMAN'S SPEECH AT COMPANY MEETING

1. Summarize each of the following paragraphs giving a brief outline of the subject matter in each.
2. Write a précis of the whole speech (about 650 words), reducing it to 200 words.

You will gather from my remarks that, compared with last year, tea and rubber realized a higher net price. Estate costs generally in Ceylon were higher, and we, in common with other owners, experienced increased production costs for both tea and rubber. Factors which contributed to this were the higher rate of exchange which, of course, affected all estate expenditure, loss on rice, increased manuring, weeding and depreciation; also, in the case of rubber, a reduction in crop.

We do not for a moment claim that our costs are anything like as low as we eventually hope to get them when our estates reach what we should describe as their normal condition. You will remember that when we took them over each of the eight estates was in a very impoverished condition, and we are having to pay the penalty for the many years of lack of care and proper cultivation prior to our assuming control. Only those with knowledge of tea-growing fully realize what a long and heavy burden such neglect entails. We are gradually overcoming the many difficulties we had to encounter, and the conditions of the respective estates show gratifying, though perhaps in some cases, slow improvements, and augur well for continued and lasting success.

With regard to manuring, the amount spent was £5,214 and is indicative of our resolve to continue high cultivation, convinced as we are that it will result in steadily increasing yields. As old neglected fields are freed from weed growth and are cleaned and redrained, they are brought into the manuring programme, so that the item of expense is a growing one in the general working, but will give commensurate returns of crops in future years, for which we must be content to wait.

The machinery on all of our estates is kept in good running order. In addition, we are at present undertaking very large improvements to the factory, comprising the addition of two new upper storeys, which will give us the requisite accommodation for the larger crops now being obtained from this property.

We have had quantity tests taken of the water supply of this estate over a long period, and find that it permits the installation of a turbine for factory power—the cheapest form of motor power there is—which will effect a material saving in the cost of manufacture when compared with the steam engine used up to now. On completion of these works we hope to turn out teas of greater value than hitherto.

The survey to which I referred at the last meeting has enabled us to have working plans of each estate, and has supplied us with authentic information relating to both our planted and unplanted areas. We are now enabled to organize properly the actual work on estates where contracts are given on an acreage basis, previously to a certain extent a matter of guesswork. Our estates consist of over 9,600 acres, of which 2,618 acres are tea, rubber, etc., in bearing.

The remaining acreage includes a considerable quantity of valuable tea-growing land, some of which, it is hoped, as labour permits, will be reclaimed. A start has already been made during the year. A forty-acre new clearing was completed, and a further ninety acres commenced. The land is all suitable, and should give good results when it reaches the bearing stage.

You will, I think, be satisfied to leave the question of what policy should be adopted, with regard to the large quantity of valuable land available for tea-growing, to the discretion of the board.

Opening new clearings is mainly dependent on the available labour, and it is unwise, therefore, to open more land unless we can secure the labour for it.

–11–

Minutes and Reports

It is important to note the difference between **Minutes** and **Reports**. The former are, in most cases, the record of actual decisions, recommendations and memoranda; the latter are written in narrative form and contain an analysis of the matter reported on, with or without recommendation.

MINUTES

These are a clear, correct and concise record of business discussed and decisions reached at a meeting. They are later approved at the next meeting of the company, club or committee as the case may be. This is done over the signature of the chairman of the meeting, after the minutes have been read out by the secretary and approved by the meeting.

N.B. In some cases the minutes may have been circulated beforehand by the secretary and, if approval of the meeting is obtained, they may "be taken as read."

For purposes of record and reference, Minutes are written up in a *Minute Book;* this record of the meeting should include the date, the time and the place of meeting. It should also give the names of those present, though this, of course, is possible only at a small meeting. Moreover it should include the exact wording of any resolutions passed, with, in the case of important resolutions, the names of proposer and seconder.

AGENDA. This is a Latin word meaning "things to be done"

and is a list of the items of business to be dealt with at a meeting. These items are arranged in logical order so that it will not be necessary to take a later item first, thus possibly affecting a decision on one of the earlier items. Routine business is always placed first to clear the way for discussion of any special items.

Study this example—

Crossland Golf Club,
Dale Green,
York, YO2 7LS
23rd February, 19..

W. Fraser Norton Esq

Dear Sir,

A meeting of Committee will be held in the Clubhouse on Saturday, 2nd March, at 5 pm.

AGENDA

1. Minutes of Committee Meeting on 10th February, 19..
2. Membership
3. Sub-Committee reports
4. Authorise payment of staff pension to R. Dobbs, Head Greenkeeper, in his retirement
5. Letter from Mr.C.F.Meston about Five-Day membership
6. Any other business

Yours faithfully,
R. Baxter
Secretary

The above is a simple and straightforward example of a club agenda. The secretary has called the meeting, given the place, the date, the time, and given notice of the items to be discussed.

The agenda for an Annual General Meeting follows similar lines—

THE BOSTOCK CHAMBER OF COMMERCE

21 Queen's Crescent
Bostock
Tel: 091-225   5617
Telex 72318

EYA/AEB   5th May, 19..

EDUCATION AND TRAINING COMMITTEE

To all members:

The Annual General Meeting of the Education and Training Committee will be held on Thursday 23rd May at 2.30 pm at 21 Queen's Crescent, Bostock.

Please let me know on the enclosed reply card whether or not you are able to attend.

                              E.Y.Arnold
                                Secretary
Enc.

AGENDA

1. Minutes
2. Matters arising
3. Correspondence
4. Chairman's Report
5. Finance
6. Election of Office Bearers
7. Joint Liaison Committee:
    (a) Teacher Visits
    (b) Work Experience for Pupils
    (c) Work Experience for Teachers
8. Next Meeting
9. Any other business

Now let us look at the *Minutes* of the above Agenda. Remember that they must be a clear and accurate record of the business discussed and decisions reached at the meeting.
They might take this form—

THE BOSTOCK CHAMBER OF COMMERCE
EDUCATION AND TRAINING COMMITTEE

Minutes of the Annual General Meeting held on Thursday 23rd May 19.. at 2.30 pm at 21 Queen's Crescent, Bostock.

PRESENT:

R.P.Brown	Chairman
W.M.Dawson	Chalmers Grammar School
W.Frame Watson	Scott College of Technology
T.R.Wooller	Ministry of Labour
T.M.White	Youth Employment Service
W.Stuart Rye	Bostock College of Commerce
A.E.Clegg	Madson, Snead & Co Ltd
T.Hunt Jones	
Miss Helen Newsome	Thos Singleton Ltd
E.Y.Arnold	Secretary
Miss Jean Crowther	Secretariat

1. MINUTES
   The Minutes of the meeting held on 14th February 19.. had been circulated; they were taken as read and signed as correct.

2. MATTERS ARISING
   There were no matters arising.

3. CORRESPONDENCE
   Apologies for absence were received from four committee members.

4. CHAIRMAN'S REPORT

The Chairman reported as follows—

The Committee had met five times during the year. Principal matters dealt with had included liaison with the local education authority. Both the Chairman and the Secretary served on the Joint Committee to establish closer contact between Schools and Industry.

The Business/Teacher Liaison Scheme had continued, and ten visits in all had been arranged for teachers.

In March the Committee had assisted with the Careers Week Exhibition during which a panel from the committee held advice-sessions on careers for schoolchildren.

5. FINANCE
The Secretary reported on the financial statement as at 31st December 19.. in respect of the fund held for the payment of medals and prizes.

The accounts recorded a further donation from Mr T.Hunt Jones of £10 for prizes at the Bostock College of Commerce.

The capital sum now stood at £199·28.
The report was accepted.

6. ELECTION OF OFFICE BEARERS
The Chairman reported that he had served his term of office and that the Vice-Convener, Mr W.Diack, was unable to accept the Chairmanship of Committee because of illness.

It was agreed to invite Mr W.Frame Watson, Principal of the Scott College of Technology, to accept the Chairmanship of Committee.

7. JOINT LIAISON COMMITTEE
   (a) The Chairman reported that ten teacher visits had been organised during the year. Headmasters had written to the secretary commenting on the success of these team-visits.

   (b) The scheme for work experience for pupils had been started. The first response from firms and industry was encouraging.

   (c) Difficulty was being found in placing teachers for work experience. An ad hoc committee was appointed to examine the reasons for this.

   Mr T. M. White (Youth Employment Service) and Mr. W. Frame Watson (Scott College of Technology) spoke of encouraging results achieved by the Liaison Committee.

8. NEXT MEETING
   This was left to the Chairman and the Secretary to arrange.

9. ANY OTHER BUSINESS
   There was none.

   Meeting terminated 4.20 pm.

You will have noticed how the Minutes of this meeting followed exactly the pattern set down in the Agenda (*see* page 143). The meeting was clearly an orderly one, and accomplished what it set out to accomplish.

Now study this example of a *Notice* calling the annual general meeting of a company—

NOTICE IS HEREBY GIVEN that the 50th Annual General Meeting of the Abacus Transport Company Limited will be held at Abacus House, London EC1, on Wednesday, 5th May 19.. at 11.30 am, for the following purposes, namely—

1. To receive and consider the Company's Accounts and the Reports of the Directors and of the Auditors for the year ended 31st December 19..

2. To declare a dividend

3. To elect Directors

4. To authorize the Board to fix the remuneration of the Auditors for 19..

5. To transact any other ordinary business

                           By Order of the Board
                           A. Snow, Secretary
10th April 19..   Abacus House, London EC1

The above is the form of Notice generally sent by companies to their shareholders. You should again note the simplicity and conciseness of the notice.

On the next page there is an example of the Minutes for such a meeting.

Study this example of the *Minutes* of a company's annual general meeting—

Minutes of the Annual General Meeting of members of the Don Metal Co Ltd, held at 7 North Wynd, Aberdeen on Wednesday 13th June 19..
Mr A. Brownlie, Chairman of the Board, presided.

1. The Secretary read the notice convening the meeting and the auditors' report.

2. The Chairman addressed the Meeeting and proposed: that the Directors' report and accounts for the year ending 31st October 19.. produced at the Meeting, be hereby received and adopted, and that a dividend of 20% less income tax be declared, to be payable to members on 30th June 19...

3. The Chairman proposed that Mr C. Davidson, the director retiring by rotation, be re-elected as a director of the Company. Mr R. Bronson seconded the motion which was put to the meeting and carried unanimously.

4. Mr P. Quentin, a shareholder, proposed that Messrs Howell, Jones & Co, having agreed to continue in office as auditors for a further year, their fee be fixed at £.... This was seconded by Mr J. Hobson, another shareholder, put to the meeting and carried unanimously.

5. There was no other business.

Technical Terms

You will not be required to know the whole range of these, but you should be familiar with the more common. Here are some you should understand—

Motion This is a formal proposal put before a meeting for the purpose of arriving at a decision. Each motion must be *moved* and *seconded*. If it is not seconded, there is no discussion on the point in question and no vote, and the motion "falls to the ground."

Amendment This is a motion to alter the terms of an original motion, normally by the addition or deletion of words. Like a motion, it must be moved and seconded. If there is a vote, the amendment must be taken first.

Resolution This is a formal decision arrived at by vote of the members at a meeting.

Rider This is an addition to a resolution after it has been passed. It adds to, but does not alter the sense of the resolution. Note carefully, therefore, its difference from an amendment. It must be proposed, seconded and voted upon.

Lie on the Table This is a motion proposing that no action be taken on a particular matter meantime; in other words, that it "should lie on the table." It may of course be raised again at a subsequent meeting.

Put the Question This is in effect the way in which the chairman announces the motion, e.g., "The question before the meeting is. . . ."

Unanimously When all members at a meeting vote in favour of a motion, the motion is said to be carried *unanimously*, i.e., *with one voice*.

Nem con This is abbreviated Latin for *nemine contradicente*, "no one contradicting." A motion is carried *nem con* when there have been no votes against, although there may have been abstentions.

Ad hoc This is a Latin phrase meaning *for this purpose*. Therefore, an *ad hoc* committee is one that has been appointed for a specific purpose, to carry out a particular aim, to report back on a special responsiblity.

EXERCISE I

1. Write a short paragraph on (*a*) Minutes and (*b*) Agenda, to show your understanding of the difference between them.
2. As secretary of your local Tennis Club, write a notice to your committee, convening a meeting and setting out the agenda.
3. Write the Minutes to the Agenda listed on page 147 for the 50th Annual General Meeting of the Abacus Transport Company Ltd, held on Wednesday 5th May 19 . .
4. Prepare the Agenda for the Annual General Meeting of the Don Metal Co, Ltd, to be held in 13th June 19 . . from the minutes given on page 148.

REPORTS

The purpose of a **Business Report** is to group together, in accurate and concise manner and with brevity, important data showing the true position of affairs relating to a particular matter. Recommendations or suggestions may or may not be made, as dictated by circumstances or under set terms of reference. Reports are in fact guides to management and organization.

A Report should be characterized by clear expression and neat display; it should be in the nature of an argument, well reasoned and arranged, accurate in detail, and leading logically to conclusions and recommendations, if any.

Here are some guide lines which you may find helpful.

(i) Observe the same rules as for the writing of business-letters, namely—clarity, accuracy, brevity.
(ii) Arrange the information or argument in logical order.
(iii) Use indirect speech, unless, of course a personal report has been specifically asked for.
(iv) Indicate the nature of the report by giving it a heading clear in meaning.
(v) Plan the lay-out of your report carefully, giving special note to headings, paragraphs, sub-paragraphs, listed points, etc.
(vi) Date and sign your report.

Reports are of two types—

   (*a*) Ordinary or Routine Reports
   (*b*) Special Reports

ORDINARY REPORTS are presented normally at set intervals and passed on routine information, e.g. chairman's report to the annual general meeting of shareholders; monthly progress reports; financial or sales reports.

They generally contain a statement of facts. Each subject should carry a separate paragraph with relevant reference or heading.

In business today much more use is being made of forms for routine report work.

SPECIAL REPORTS are what they say, namely, reports of a special inquiry, e.g. on accidents, fire-damage, staffing, etc. They may also be reports from a sub-committee appointed for the specific purpose of examining an item or requirement and reported back to a main committee or authority.

The content of any Special Report is determined by its *Terms of Reference*, i.e. the instruction or guide governing the report; in many cases such terms of reference come direct from the Minute Book.

In the writing of a Special Report the Terms of Reference should be stated first; facts and arguments should then follow in logical order and all such facts and arguments must be relevant to such Terms of Reference; then come the findings; and finally the conclusions and recommendations.

The Report must be signed and dated.

N.B. In the writing of Reports always be logical and relevant and do not show your own bias.

On the next page there is an example of a Special Report.

	Report of Sub-Committee on the Siting of two additional shelters in the Botanical Gardens
Terms of Reference	By a resolution passed at the Parks & Gardens Committee Meeting on 4th March, the sub-committee was instructed to examine the siting possibilities for two additional shelters in the Botanical Gardens.
Action by Sub-Committee	Three meetings were held — on 9th, 17th and 25th March. Two of these were held in the Gardens where possible sites were examined. The Parks' surveyor, Mr G. Small, was present on both occasions; his report is attached.
Findings	(i) Several good sites are available, two in the South Garden and one in the Palm Grove, as shown on the enclosed plan at (A), (B), and (C). (ii) All three are suitable, but siting at (B) would result in the loss of some very valuable shrubs.
Recommendations	That one shelter be sited in the South Garden at (A), the other at (C) in the Palm Grove.
Encls	(Signed) James Clarke Convener.

MINUTES AND REPORTS

A MEMORANDUM or memo is a short and informal note, report or message, generally written on a specially printed form.

It is used mostly for brief intimations, e.g. dispatch of goods, receipt of formal communications, appointments, etc, within departments of a business.

Printed forms vary, but follow this pattern—

MEMORANDUM

From: Sales Manager
Ref: SM/141/A   To: Advertising Manager
                     Date: 17.11.19..

Attached report for your comments, by
            30/11 please.
Encl.   SM.

COLLEGE INTER-BRANCH MEMO

From: FM   To: CS   Ref: Stationery
                Date: 19.10.19..

Let me know present stock of letter head pads; Newcastle are asking for two gross.
                                              FM.

EXERCISE II

1. What is a Business Report? How does it differ from Minutes?
2. Write the report of a sub-committee appointed to investigate rowdyism at a recent Club Dance; you are the secretary of the club.
3. Your employer wishes to close the firm's canteen. He states that it is not being patronized and that he would prefer to

issue luncheon vouchers. He asks you to write a report on the situation and to make recommendations. Write this report.
4. Write a memo from the Manager of a firm to the Personnel Officer asking for information on the progress of the Staff Welfare Scheme.
5. You have been asked to look into the sharp rise in the use of stationery in your office over the past three months. Write your report to the office manager.
6. Your employer has decided to keep the office open during lunch by staggering the lunch hours. Write him a memo showing how this can be done.

–12–

Comprehension Exercises

Comprehension and interpretation of a passage means understanding and explaining what is written in the passage. Interpretation goes much further than paraphrasing; nevertheless, successful interpretation depends largely upon the ability to paraphrase.

Paraphrasing has been described as "expressing in one's own words something that an author has said very much better in his." You will find this a good guide to interpretation, for in interpretation you should deliberately make a personal paraphrase, not necessarily in writing, of each phrase and sentence in the passage set for exercise. In this way intelligent reading is assured, and, at the same time, you will find that the answers to certain questions being asked are being framed naturally "in your own words."

Here are some guide-lines to help you—

1. Read the passage carefully and slowly, more than once; if possible read it aloud.
2. At your second or third reading, make a personal paraphrase, in your mind, of each sentence.
3. Read the questions set, paying close attention to the exact requirements of each.
4. Locate the section of the passage that gives authority for each answer. The material used in your answer must be found in the given subject matter, except when a personal opinion is asked for.

5. Always answer in properly constructed sentences, and, unless instructed otherwise, in your own words. Single words or short phrases from the original, however, if simple and in common use, may be used.
6. When asked to give the meaning of words and phrases as used in the passage, make sure that what you set down can be substituted for the original. In this type of answer, sentence form is not necessary. But do try to be neat and use lists.
7. If asked to suggest a title to the passage, leave this answer until the other questions have been attempted; by doing this you should find it easier to provide an appropriate title.
8. Consult your dictionary for the meaning of an unfamiliar word.

Here is a passage followed by some comprehension questions. The answers are given on the following page. Try, at first, to answer the questions on your own without referring to the answers. Then use the answers I have given to check your answers.

Discovery

The land was now clearly seen about two leagues distant. Whereupon they took in sail and laid to, waiting impatiently for the dawn. The thoughts and feelings of Columbus in this little space of time must have been confused and intense. At length, in spite of every difficulty and danger, he had **accomplished his object.** The great mystery of the ocean was revealed; his theory, which had been the scoff of sages, was triumphantly established; he had secured to himself **a glory durable as the world itself.** It is difficult to conceive the feelings of such a man, at such a moment; or the conjectures which must have thronged upon his mind as to the land before him, covered with darkness. That it was fruitful was evident from the vegetables which floated from its shores. He thought, too, that he perceived the fragrance of aromatic groves. The moving light he had beheld proved it the residence of man. But what were its inhabitants? Were they like those of the other parts of the globe; or were they some strange

COMPREHENSION EXERCISES 157

and monstrous race, such as the imagination was prone in those times to give to all remote and unknown regions? Had he come upon some wild island far in the Indian Sea; or was this the famed Cipango itself, **the object of his golden fancies? A thousand speculations of the kind** must have swarmed upon him, as, with his anxious crews, he waited for the night to pass away, wondering whether the morning light would reveal a savage wilderness, or dawn upon spicy groves and glittering faces and gilded cities, and all the splendour of oriental civilization.

(by Washington Irving)

1. What words or phrases in the passage show that Columbus thought he might have reached the Far East?
2. What were the causes of doubt and confusion in Columbus's mind as he waited for dawn?
3. Of what facts concerning the new land could Columbus be sure and why?
4. From your reading of the passage, what do you understand to have been the life's ambition of Columbus?
5. From your general knowledge of Columbus, what was his theory about "the great mystery of the ocean"? and why was it "the scoff of sages"?
6. Explain in your own words the meaning of each of the following phrases—
    (a) "accomplished his object"
    (b) "a glory durable as the world itself"
    (c) "the object of his golden fancies"
    (d) "a thousand speculations of the kind"

Your answers might follow this pattern—
1. The words and phrases in the passage that show us that Columbus thought he might have reached the Far East are—
    (a) "he thought he perceived the fragrance of aromatic groves"
    (b) "was this the famed Cipango itself, object of his golden fancies?"

(c) "wondering whether the morning light would ... dawn upon spicy groves and glittering faces and gilded cities, and all the splendour of oriental civilization."

2. Columbus was confused and doubtful because land could be seen about seven miles off, but it was night time and in the dark he could only guess as to the nature of the land they had discovered. The light of dawn would bring certainty.

3. Columbus was sure that the land was fertile because he could see vegetables floating from its shores. He was also sure that there was human habitation on the land, as he had seen a moving light. Of more he could not be sure.

4. From reading the passage, I think that Columbus's main ambition in life was to discover Cipango, or Japan, referred to in the passage as "the object of his golden fancies."

5. Columbus had a theory that the earth was a sphere and that this could be proved if he discovered Asia by sailing West rather than East. This theory was "the scoff of sages" because the wise men of the time believed that the world was flat.

6. (a) succeeded in his aim
   (b) a triumph which would last as long as the world existed
   (c) the place he wished above all to see
   (d) innumerable similar speculations

Now try to answer the questions on the following passages in the same way.

Hollywood—the New Tycoons

Gazing bleakly out over a decaying studio lot cluttered with the relics of past epics, the veteran movie executive heaved a deep sigh and muttered something about a ghost town.

This is Hollywood, 1970, the dream factory where five of the seven major film companies lost a total of something like $150m last year. The movie capital of the world, where only one of every six films distributed in the United States is now made and where "for sale" signs are going up on the great studios. Where more than 40 per cent of the industry's craft workers are unemployed and star-studded Beverly Hills is being called a "disaster area" as a massive **austerity programme** begins to bite.

Paradoxically, while Hollywood suffers, the rest of the movie business is doing pretty well. Although attendance slipped a bit last year, box office receipts hit a seven-year peak at over $1,000m and new cinemas are opening at a very healthy rate. But in the space of little more than two years, the face of the industry has been transformed. And it has not been a **bloodless revolution.** Burdened by tight money, **hamstrung by management** and, above all, culturally incapable of recognizing fundamental changes in their market, most of the major studios have paid the price and are now scrabbling frantically to get back on the **gravy train.**

The most dramatic illustration of Hollywood's troubles is there for all to see. Endless all-weather queues for *Easy Rider, Medium Cool* and *Midnight Cowboy,* which together cost about $5m to make. Half-empty cinemas for lavish, big-name films like *Dr. Doolittle* (cost $18m), *Goodbye Mr. Chips* (over $19m) and *Star* ($13m). This is not the whole story—television's fierce competition and hair-raising operating costs are important factors—but the underlying reason for the financial crisis which the industry now faces can be traced back to Hollywoods's disastrous complacency.

Apparently unaware—or perhaps simply uncaring—that almost 70 per cent of all movie-goers are now under 24, the industry continued to operate as if it was still catering for the safe predictable and lost audience of the over-30s. "Movies are irrefutably a **youth market** just as television is irrefutably an older market," says Metro-Goldwyn-Mayer's new president, James Aubrey (former boss of C.B.S. Television). Realism, social and political content and contemporary relevance are what this better educated and more idealistic audience will stand in line for.

Victims of Hollywood's self-created glamorous myths and, surely, an inbuilt contempt for their audiences' intelligence, the major film groups missed the bus. The **conglomerates** that have moved in on them may not know much about making good movies but they can at least see through the whole sprawling mess of agents, unions, public relations and sheer ballyhoo to the real issues.

From *The Times Business News*

1. What do you understand by the term "Hollywood"?
2. Describe, in your own words, the troubles facing Hollywood.
3. What does the writer say are the causes of Hollywood's problems?
4. What does the writer suggest will be the future of Hollywood? Use quotations from the passage to support your answer.
5. What do you understand by the following words and phrases?
    (a) "austerity programme"
    (b) "bloodless revolution"
    (c) "hamstrung by management"
    (d) "gravy train"
    (e) "youth market"
    (f) "conglomerates"
6. Who were the "victims of Hollywood's self-created glamorous myths"? Explain what you think the writer means in that sentence.
7. What are the "real issues" referred to in the last sentence?

In Search of Silence

People have been sensitive to environment for a long time; they have been concerned to isolate themselves from cold and excessive heat, have insisted on adequate light, and have concerned themselves with satisfactory furniture, space to move and air to breathe. They have reacted to excessive draughts and have established **rule-of-thumb ideas** regarding ventilation. But until recently in Britain they have been amazingly unaware of the need for a good acoustical environment in which they can hear easily and clearly, in which noise is insufficient to make them deaf, and **sufficiently unobtrusive** not to distract them from their tasks.

The reason for this is simple; ears are amazingly adaptive to large ranges of sound levels, people do not notice deafness in themselves for many years, and the ear is able to recognize speech in a surprisingly high level of noise. Noise energy from a machine can often be doubled without the growth being clearly recognized, so that over the years an **insidious worsening of noise environment** has been going on without the outcry which would have occurred if the same had happened with warmth, lighting or smell.

In general, the increasing fight for industrial competitiveness has doubled the power of aircraft, cars, electrical equipment and industrial tools every five to 10 years, This power has been obtained from small (and therefore cheaper), faster-moving machinery, and offices, lecture rooms and homes of lighter materials have been built closer than ever to sources of noise. Unfortunately, noise increases generally with horse-power used, with the tip speeds of moving parts, and with the flimsiness of the walls of the machines or ducts in which air flows. As a result noise entering offices and houses from diesel lorries and cars along busy main roads is so great that windows have to be closed and double glazing must be fitted.

In the centre of London where streets are rapidly developing into **deep chasms** this noise nuisance extends upwards to the highest office, the effect of distance being more than outweighed by the greater length of roadway unshielded by other buildings. Similarly in the field of aviation the number of people disturbed from aircraft landing and taking off is increasing rapidly around Heathrow airport: the number now approaches 400,000, more than the total population of many cities. In factories deafness to some degree or other is commonplace. Even so, there are as yet no anti-noise regulations nor is compensation payable to sufferers.

From *The Times*.

1. What do you understand by the term "environment"?
2. Explain in you own words why people are "unaware of the need for a good acoustical environment."
3. Explain the distinction the author makes between our sense of hearing and our awareness of warmth, lighting and smell.
4. What accounts for the increased level of noise in modern life?
5. What, do you think, are the dangers to people of excessive noise?
6. Can excessive noise be avoided? If so, how? If not, why not?

7. Explain in your own words the meaning of the following words and phrases—
   (a) "rule-of-thumb ideas"
   (b) "sufficiently unobtrusive"
   (c) "insidious worsening"
   (d) "deep chasms"

The Voyage of the 'Discovery'

On the following day with cheerful sunshine to aid our efforts we proceeded for some way up the bed of a frozen stream, still on the south side of the glacier. On our right was the glacier itself, **distorted with a mass of wall faces** and **pinnacles which looked unscaleable**, whilst on our left were the steep bare hillsides; soon the glacier stream came to an end, and we were forced to consider what was next to be done. As a result of our consultation some of the party climbed the hillside **to prospect,** while Skelton and I attacked the glacier. We fully expected to discover a mass of broken ice extending right across the inlet, but were agreeably surprised to find that by carefully selecting our route we could work our way to the **summit of the disturbance**; and secondly that beyond our immediate neighbourhood, the high sharp ice hillocks settled down into more gradual ridges. This implied that to the north things were smoother, and after our short **reconnaissance** and a confirming report from the hills, we occupied the rest of the day in carrying out loads and sledges in the direction we had chosen across the disturbance. It was a **difficult portage** but by night we were camped in a small dip well in the glacier surface.

From *Voyage of the 'Discovery'* by Robert Falcon Scott

1. Write an account of the day's activities for the expedition's log-book.
2. What words and phrases in the passage suggest that the party was exploring the area for the first time?
3. What was the main problem facing the explorers on this day?

4. How was the problem eventually overcome?
5. Why do you think the author describes the sunshine as being "cheerful?"
6. Describe in your own words the glacier as it appeared to the explorers.
7. Explain the meaning of the following words and phrases.
    (a) "distorted with a mass of wall faces"
    (b) "pinnacles which looked unscaleable"
    (c) "to prospect"
    (d) "the summit of the disturbance"
    (e) "reconnaissance"
    (f) "difficult portage"

Putting a Boffin on the Board

Top Management scientists should be on company boards, Martin Blackburn, managing director of the Touche Ross management consultants firm, told the United Kingdom Chapter of the Institute of Management Scientists at their spring meeting at the University of Sussex yesterday. Perhaps surprisingly his suggestion was not greeted with great joy by the assembled potential directors.

One man thought that companies still preferred to recruit generals, peers and politicians when bringing in **non-executive directors.** Others were generally gloomy about the prospect of management scientists reaching such heights.

Management science is a relatively new profession in this country and the grafting of a management services section on to our large companies has not always been an **unalloyed** success, as the instance of International Publishing Corporation indicates. Mr. Blackburn did not deal with specific examples yesterday, but he did lay down some general principles for the success of manament services teams, which are in effect **internal management consultancies.**

The first essential, he felt, was for a **high-calibre** head of the team whose word carried weight throughout the company. If not on the board, he needed to have direct access to the chairman.

By and large this kind of access is much easier for the outside consultant.

Independence was another essential, and Mr. Blackburn interpreted this as meaning no **line responsibilities,** not even for the computer which in practice is very often lumped with management services. The team needs high-calibre men not failed line managers. It needs a broad range of skills and sufficient initiative to make suggestions to management without waiting for projects to be handed out. Finally, Mr. Blackburn feels that management services should be profitable and should charge a fee for its services to group companies.

From *The Times Business News*

1. What do you understand by the term "management science"?
2. Why do you suppose the suggestion that Top Management scientists should be on company boards was not greeted with enthusiasm?
3. What do you consider would be the task of a management service team once it was "grafted" onto a large company?
4. Why do you suppose "the grafting of a management services section onto our large companies" has not always been successful?
5. What suggestions were made for the success of mangement services teams?
6. What do you understand by the following words and phrases?
    (*a*) "non-executive directors"
    (*b*) "unalloyed"
    (*c*) "internal management consultancies"
    (*d*) "high-calibre"
    (*e*) "line responsibilities"

Violence on Screen

There seems little reason to be too alarmed at the extent of swearing and sex on British television. Swearing in any case is more likely to be **distasteful** than corrupting unless there is a deliberate attempt to shock and disgust. There seems to be no evidence of this. Some of the language may seem ill chosen but some **latitude** must be allowed for the sake of realism, and therefore the **artistic integrity** of a programme, and also for the standards commonly observed in everyday life. Sexual **titillation** on television is potentially more dangerous in that it can influence as well as reflect the normally accepted standards of conduct and can certainly be embarrassing for family viewing. But again the survey would not justify any alarmist conclusions.

The findings on violence are certainly more worrying. There is no indication of anything like the orgy of brutality to which American viewers are regularly subjected. Violence still forms a small proportion of British television watching both in quantity and quality. But there does seem to be a certain amount of violence which is not demanded by the nature of the programme. The distinction is crucial. It means that news programmes of bloodshed and brutality should be judged differently from fiction. Of course there can be the calculated and unnecessary attempt to shock the viewer in news programmes as in any other. But sometimes the shock in necessary for the sake of **objective** news coverage. A bloody war cannot be adequately reported to the sound of marching bands. It is the function of a news service, whether in print, on radio, or on television, to report what has happened and there must always be the gravest misgivings about any suggestion that any item of news should ever be withheld for fear of giving offence—whether that offence is to taste or to political opinion.

It is a different matter where programmes of fiction are concerned. Sometimes episodes of violence are either so fictional and stylized as to be quite unreal or are a necessary and **integral** part of the story. They can be justified then on the basis of artistic convention or merit, and serious violence of this nature is likely to be so infrequent as not to constitute much of a danger. But there is quite a bit of realistic television violence for its own sake— violence which shocks and which then, even more important, may accustom the viewer to sights of brutality as part of ordinary life. This occurs now mostly in American programmes, but soon old films will become available to television containing far more violence than those now being shown. The danger does not come therefore from programmes made in Britian, but that can be no defence for British television authorities. Their responsibility is for what is shown and one must assume that violence can be advertised as effectively as any other product.

From *The Times*

1. What reasons are given for not being too alarmed at the extent of swearing and sex on British television?
2. What cause is there, if any, for concern at the violence on British television?
3. What kind of violence is dangerous on television? Why is it dangerous?
4. When is the showing of violence on television justified and why?
5. Who is responsible for the violence shown on British television and why?
6. Summarize in one paragraph the writer's attitude towards violence on British television.
7. Give another word for each of the following—
   (*a*) "distasteful"
   (*b*) "latitude"
   (*c*) "artistic integrity"
   (*d*) "titillation"
   (*e*) "objective"
   (*f*) "integral"

The Tycoon's World

If you are a **breathless young businessman** on the make, half-way to your first million pounds, you need a telephone in your car, Girl Fridays about the place and a business jet at London airport. The idea is that tycoons must spend as much of their time on tycoonery as possible. They must not dissipate it by driving themselves up to Birmingham. They must not waste it in airport lounges. Secretaries or electronic equivalents must always be available—no question of hanging about waiting for your girl to come back from lunch-time shopping in Oxford Street. Thus a whole new industry has sprung up which specialises in services, **gadgets and gimmickry for whiz-kids.**

Here are some of the facilities currently available. Arriving at Heathrow on a scheduled flight, first class, **our young tycoon** changes into his own jet. If you hire it from Executive Jet Aviation the cost is £1 per mile, £200 minimum charge per flight. The Lear jet has seats for six passengers, plus pilot and co-pilot. Unfortunately no hostesses are provided—you have to bring your own. The sales argument is that private jet travel is essential for 'men to whom a matter of minutes can make the difference between failure and success.' Well, I wonder about that. Do many business deals depend upon split-second timing? I must also issue a warning. None of the business jets in which I have travelled are at all comfortable. It is speed and convenience you are buying rather than luxury.

There are about 1,000 business jets in use throughout the world. Of these, 900 are in America and only about fifty in Europe. To buy a business jet can cost up to £300,000 plus the high cost of airport charges, maintenance facilities and the employment of two internationally qualified pilots. It is, therefore, sometimes more economic to hire a jet than purchase one. Executive Jet Aviation's 550 mph Lear jets are spread throughout Europe and can be summoned at any time by Telex, or through a telephone call with the aid of a special identity card. EJA is even willing to put the customer's name on the side of the plane.

From the *Spectator*

1. Do you think the writer is serious or not? Give reasons for your answer.
2. How would you describe the writer's attitude to "tycoonery"?
3. Give your definition of "tycoonery."
4. Comment on the writer's use of the following words and phrases.
    (a) "breathless young businessman."

(b) "gadgets and gimmickry for whiz-kids."
   (c) "our young tycoon."
5. What is the writer's opinion of private jet travel? What are the reasons given for this view?
6. Think up another title for this excerpt.

The Nature of Management

Management has, of course, been practised since the dawn of human history. Men have always collaborated with one another in hunting and building and agriculture and many other activities. Such collaboration for a common end implies arrangements for a division of labour, which in turn **postulates the existence of a leader**—someone whose task it is both to make the arrangements and to see that the remainder of the group carries them out. Where the group is a very simple one, there may be no formal appointment of a leader. Everyone knows what his job is and how it fits in with the other man's job; he regards it as natural and inevitable that he should play his part in the group. Such things are dictated by **immemorial custom**, the folk-ways of family or tribe rooted in the **unconscious accumulation of experience**, the leaf-drift of the centuries.

But even among primitive groups there were **originals**, people who did not want to work or who wanted to work in ways different from those laid down by tradition. If there had not been such people there could have been no progress in man's knowledge and mastery over his environment. They were, however, regarded as a nuisance; they wanted to disturb the **habit patterns** of the rest of the group, the comfortable working arrangements which everyone understood and to which they were accustomed. There were also quarrelsome people, men who wanted other men's wives, or ornaments or other possessions: they, too, upset the orderly social life of the group.

Out of these necessities man evolved the institution of *leadership*. Individuals, because of their age, or knowledge of the customs of the group, or superior strength or cunning which made others afraid of them, acquired authority. They became the leaders of their groups. People did what such men told them to do. Where this authority was supported by the general feeling of the group it was much more powerful than when it rested solely on fear. But whatever its foundation, it served to hold the group together, to enable men and women to **collaborate** in tasks of various kinds without disturbance of the social patterns they had evolved.

From *The Nature of Management* by H. R. Light

1. The writer suggests two ways in which leaders emerge in primitive types of society. What are they?
2. Which was the most powerful kind of leadership and why?
3. Why was it necessary in some kinds of primitive society to appoint a leader?
4. Explain the meaning within the context of the passage of the following words and phrases
    (a) "postulates the existence of a leader"
    (b) "immemorial custom"
    (c) "unconscious accumulation of experience"
    (d) "originals"
    (e) "habit patterns"
    (f) "collaborate"
5. Explain in your own words the function of a leader in primitive society.

The Man with the Magic Touch

What is a "journalist"? Many ambiguities surround his title and his functions. **To seize truth by the hair** as it hurries past, recognize it instantly and **set it down in broad sure strokes,** calls for qualities which derive equally from study and from contact with the world. Ideally the journalist should be something of a teacher, a detective and a showman. And of an artist, too, for his picture of events must reveal what is significant without fussy and obscuring detail. The journalist is a man trained **to go to the heart of the matter.**

Journalism, however, is not a profession which admits of exact definition. To qualify as a lawyer or a doctor takes years of study, but a man may become a "journalist" sometimes after comparatively brief experience. For while the political and social judgement he needs cannot be acquired in a day, **a sense of news values is partly intuitive.** You have it, or you have it not. If you have it at all you can develop it by practice.

Here are two views on the subject, both expressed by distinguished journalists. Mr. R. D. Blumenfeld, editor of the *Daily Express* from 1902 to 1932, said that in Georgian times, as today, the person who procured, prepared and published the news was the journalist; the foundation stone of the newspaper structure. The news sheet, lacking his magic touch, would fail without hope of recovery. The journalist "makes" the newspaper. Mr. Wickham Steed, editor of *The Times* from 1919 to 1922, wrote this about the functions of journalism—

> The ideal journalist would be one who having mastered and assimilated the wisdom of the ancients, the philosophies of the more modern, the knowledge of the scientists, the mechanics of engineers, the history of his own and of other times and the chief factors in economic, social and political life, should be able to hide all these things in his bosom and to supply as much of them as might be readily digested to his millions of readers in proportion as he divined their desire for them.

The man with the magic touch, the man of knowledge, tempering his seeming omniscience to the mental digestion of his readers, all this is well enough. But every journalist is something more—and less—than this. He is the man who traces, checks and assesses, and writes the news.

From *Mansfield's Complete Journalist* by F. J. Mansfield

1. Why is it difficult to define a "journalist"?
2. Do you think it appropriate to describe a journalist as "something of a teacher, a detective and a showman"? Give reasons for your opinion.
3. What do you understand by the following phrases?
    (a) "To seize truth by the hair"
    (b) "set it down in broad sure strokes"

    (c) "to go to the heart of the matter"
    (d) "A sense of news values is partly intuitive"
4. Is the writer saying that journalists are born and not made? Give reasons for your answer.
5. What is your opinion of Mr. Wickham Steed's description of the ideal journalist?
6. What is your opinion of the standards of journalism today?

Business as Usual

'I wonder if you could come down next weekend?'
 'I'm in conference all Tuesday.'
'Wednesday, then?'
 'I'd be delighted. Could you pick me up at the club?'
'Athenaeum?'
 'My dear fellow, no, that Heathrow place. I'll be flying in: conference in Geneva.'
 'What flight?'
 'My own—I've just got a most interesting new swing-wing.'
 'VTOL?'
 'Hardly—a new method we'll be marketing quite soon.'
 'I'll send a Rolls.'
 'How can we contact you?'
 'My cars are fully equipped. You just call PRO/PD on your radio—the wavelength is in the international confidential file: I presume you have it?'
 'My organisation prints it.'
 'Fine, Wednesday then; bring your golf clubs.'
 'I'll get a set when I turn up.'
 'But, my dear chap, can you manage without your own?'
 'They'll be my own—VK47 Jackobusters. He designed them for me, now they're on the market.'

The Sussex cottage stood in its owner's grounds, which were not small since he had bought up three surrounding farms to ensure a proper seclusion. The private heliport on what had been the village cricket field was for some reason still resented. As the Rolls crossed the invisible beam the wrought-iron gates slid noiselessly open while the plastic coats of arms which adorned them were discreetly illuminated from inside. The Georgian front dated back to at least 1928 and behind it in parts of the house there still were traces of its sixteenth century origins. As Sir Herbert was assisted from the Rolls, the front door was opened. Bunbelly, the travelling butler, who always did for Sir William at weekends, bowed comfortably. Sir Herbert was offered a wash. (There was only a rather small and indifferent Picasso in the loo, he noticed.)

From the *Spectator*

1. How would you describe the humour in this passage?
2. At which elements of the business world does the writer poke fun?
3. How does the writer poke fun at the top-level business executives? Try to describe his method.
4. What is the effect of the dialogue? Do you think it successful or not? Give your reasons.
5. Choose three short extracts from the passage and say why you think they are funny.
6. Do you think that the writer is being fair in his picture of business men at work?
7. Invent your own title for this passage.

–13–

Abbreviations, and Foreign Words and Phrases

ABBREVIATIONS

General

AD	*Anno domini*—in the year of our Lord
ad lib	At your pleasure; as much as you like
advt	Advertisement
am	*Ante meridiem*—before noon
Anon	Anonymous
Ans	Answer
Asst	Assistant
BC	Before Christ: British Columbia (Canada)
BEA	British European Airways
BOAC	British Overseas Airways Corporation
BR	British Rail
BRS	British Road Services
C	Centigrade (thermometer scale); cent; a hundred
cf *or* cp	Compare
chq	Cheque
Co	Company; County
Dept	Department
ditto; do	The same
DV	*Deo volente*—god willing
eg	*Exempli gratia*—for (the sake of) example
Enc; Encl	Enclosure
etc	*Et cetera*—and the rest
et seq	*Et sequentia*—and the following

F	Fahrenheit (thermometer scale)
fcp	Foolscap (13 in by 8 in)
fo	Folio—a sheet of paper or two opposite pages numbered as one
HO	Head Office
Hon Sec	Honorary Secretary
hp	Horse-power; Hire Purchase
ib, ibid	*Ibidem*—in the same place
ie	*Id est*—that is
infra dig	Beneath one's dignity
JP	Justice of the Peace
M	*Monsieur*—sir
MM	Messieurs—sirs, gentlemen (Messrs)
Memo, Mem	Memorandum
MO	Money Order; Medical Officer
MP	Member of Parliament; Military Police
mph	Miles per hour
MSS	Manuscripts (sing. MS)
mth, mths	Month, months
MV	Motor Vessel
NB	*Nota bene*—take careful note
NP	Notary Public
OHMS	On Her Majesty's Service
p, pp	page, pages
PA	Personal Assistant
P/A	Power of Attorney
pc	Post card
PC	Privy Councillor; Police Constable
pl	Plural
pm	*Post meridiem*—after noon
PM	Prime Minister
PO	Postal Order; Post Office
pro	For, on behalf of
PRO	Public Relations Officer
pro tem	*Pro tempore*—for the time being
PS	*Post scriptum*—postscript, added after the signature to a letter.
PPS	A second postscript

QC	Queen's Counsel
qv	*Quod vide* which see; to which you should refer
recd	Received
ref	Reference
Rev	Reverend
Rly, Ry	Railway
RSVP	Répondez s'il vous plaît—reply, if you please
Sec, Secy	Secretary
Senr	Senior
Soc	Society
SS	Steamship
stg	Sterling
Supt	Superintendent
VIP	Very Important Person

Commercial

@	At
A1	First class (at Lloyds)
a/c	Account
ad val	*Ad valorem*—according to value
Agt	Agent
amt	Amount
A/S	Account Sales
av	Average
B/E	Bill of Exchange
b/f	Brought forward
B/L	Bill of Lading
B of E	Bank of England
Bros	Brothers
B/S	Balance Sheet
c & f	Cost and freight
cif	Cost, insurance and freight
C/N	Credit note
c/o	Care of
COD	Cash on Delivery
C/P	Charter party
Cr	Credit; creditor

CR	Company's risk
cum div	With dividend
D/A	Documents against acceptance or Documents attached
d/d	Days after date
Dis	Discount
Div	Dividend
D/N	Debit Note
D/O	Delivery Order
Dr	Debtor
E&OE	Errors and omissions excepted
ex div	Without dividend
faa	Free of all average
fas	Free alongside ship
fpa	Free of particular average
fob	Free on board
for	Free on rail
fwd	Forward
G/A	General average
in trans	*In transitu*—on the way
Inc	Incorporated
Insce	Insurance
inv	Invoice
IOU	I owe you
L/C	Letter of Credit
Ltd	Limited
m/s	Months after sight
OR	Owner's Risk
P/C	Prices current
per pro *or* pp	*Per procurationem*—on behalf of
P/N	Promissory Note
PP	Parcel Post
PTO	Please turn over
Qto or 4to	*Quarto*—folded in four
Rct	Receipt
R/D	Refer to drawer
regd	registered
$	Dollars

SAE	Stamped addressed envelope
TMO	Telegraph Money Order
8vo	*Octavo*—folded in eight
16mo	Folded in sixteen

Geographical

Bucks	Buckinghamshire
Cambs	Cambridgeshire
Cantab	Of Cambridge University
Carm	Carmarthenshire
CI	Channel Islands
Glam	Glamorganshire
Glos	Gloucestershire
Hants	Hampshire
Herts	Hertfordshire
Ill	Illinois
IOM	Isle of Man
IOW	Isle of Wight
Lancs	Lancashire
Mass	Massachussetts
Middx	Middlesex
Mon	Monmouthshire
Northants	Northamptonshire
Notts	Nottinghamshire
Oxon	Of Oxford; Oxfordshire
Salop	Shropshire
Som	Somerset
Staffs	Staffordshire
Wilts	Wiltshire
Warks	Warwickshire
Worcs	Worcestershire

FOREIGN WORDS AND PRASES

(F) French, (L) Latin

Ad valorem (L)	According to value
Agenda (L)	A list of things to be done
Ante (L)	Before

Bona fide (L)	In good faith
Bon marché (F)	Cheap
Carte blanche (F)	A free hand; full discretionary powers
Coup d'état (F)	A sudden stroke of (state) policy
Data (L)	Facts given from which other facts may be deduced
De facto (L)	From the fact
Dies non (L)	No legal day i.e. a day on which no legal business may be transacted
Ex (L)	Out of
Ex gratia (L)	Without prejudice
Ex officio (L)	By virtue of office
Gratis (L)	Without payment
In camera (L)	In a (judge's) private chambers
In extenso (L)	In full
In toto (L)	In the whole; entirely
Inter alia (L)	Among other things
Ipso facto (L)	In the fact itself; virtually
Locum tenens (L)	Deputy; acting
Locus standi (L)	A place for standing; a right to interfere
Nil desperandum (L)	Never despair
Nulli secundus (L)	Second to none
Obiter dictum (L)	A cursory remark
Pari passu (L)	With equal pace; together
Per (L)	Through an agency
Per contra (L)	On the other side
Persona grata (L)	A welcome person
Post mortem (L)	After death
Poste Restante (F)	To be kept in P.O. until fetched
Prima facie (L)	On the face of it; at first sight
Pro (L)	For; on behalf of
Pro forma (L)	As a matter of form
Pro rata (L)	In proportion
Quid pro quo (L)	Value for Value
Quorum (L)	Number of members required to make decisions binding
Quota (L)	The part of share assigned to each
Sine die (L)	Indefinitely

Sine qua non (L)	An indispensable condition
Status quo (L)	Unchanged position
Stet (L)	Let it stand
Sub judice (L)	Under consideration
Sub rosa (L)	Privately
Tempus fugit (L)	Time flies
Ultra vires (L)	Beyond one's legal powers
Verbatim (L)	Word for word
Via (L)	By way of
Vice (L)	In place of
Vice versa (L)	The terms being exchanged
Videlicet (Viz) (L)	Namely
Vis-à-vis (F)	Opposite; facing
Viva voce (L)	Orally

–14–

Test Papers

TEST No 1

1. Correct, where necessary, these sentences; explain the reasons for your corrections.
   (a) Whom do you believe him to be?
   (b) He is more business-like than me.
   (c) Neither the manufacturer nor the wholesaler were to blame.
   (d) You must forbid him coming.
   (e) I always have and always will deal with Smith & Sons.
   (f) I should be glad if you will reply at once.

2. Write sentences, one for each word, to show that you understand the difference in meaning between the words in each pair—
   (a) uninterested; disinterested
   (b) perpetrate; perpetuate
   (c) luxurious; luxuriant
   (d) annoy; aggravate
   (e) practical; practicable
   (f) affect; effect

3. Convert the following into indirect speech, beginning with the words—

   "The Chairman said that . . ."

   I must once more warn stockholders that although the purchase price of the undertaking has at last been settled, it is even yet not possible to estimate what amount will be available for distribution. I have already mentioned the complex question of taxation arising out of the sale of the undertaking and it may be that a claim or claims will be made in this country and in Malaysia in respect of capital profit.

4. Write a well-constructed paragraph of approximately 100 words on the main elements of a good business letter.

   Then write a sample business letter ordering various items from a firm in Ireland.

5. (a) You have received an opening order to the value of £200 and have been given the name of a firm as reference—
   (i) write the status enquiry to the firm (supply names and addresses)
   (ii) write the status reply (favourable)
   (b) A firm of manufacturers in Scotland is sending you one of its directors to attend the Canadian Trade Fair in Toronto in order to promote sales. Write a letter of introduction to a firm in Toronto on behalf of the director (supply names and address)

6. Write to a firm of travel agents for details of a day's motor coach tour for your firm's annual staff outing. Give details.
   Also write the reply from the firm.

TEST No 2

1. (a) Give a synonym for each of the following words—

   despatch   achieve   plan
   assent   construct apparent

   (b) Give an antonym for each of the following words—

   sever   assemble illicit
   calm   general   careful

2. Using your knowledge of grammar and style, comment on each of the following pairs—
   (a) A pocket watch/A watch pocket
   (b) Man is vile/The man is vile

182 ENGLISH FOR BUSINESS

(c) He only borrowed the books for a few days/He borrowed the books for a few days only

(d) The amenity of our streets is recommended to your care/Please keep our streets tidy

3. In a brief sentence, indicate the use of—

sub judice, ex officio, sine die, persona non grata.

(b) Give the abbreviations for—

bill of exchange, bill of lading, document against acceptance, charter party, compare, manuscript.

4. You are an applicant for a position as a shorthand-typist, and are being interviewed. Give the conversation you think would take place between you and your prospective employer.

5. Write a letter to a firm advising them that goods ordered by you have not arrived to date; urge them to give immediate attention to the order.

Write their reply.

6. Your employer has become Secretary and Treasurer to a small professional association which has just been formed. He asks you to write the following letters for his signature—

(a) to the local station hotel for the use of a room for the inaugural meeting; a meal will be required.

(b) to the firm's printers, explaining the situation, and asking for samples and quotations for the supply of notepaper and envelopes.

Invent a name for the association.

TEST No 3

1. (a) Use the following words in sentences to distinguish their meaning clearly—

deprecate   differ   precise
depreciate   defer   concise

(b) What prepositions should follow—

admit, averse, cognisant, different, militate, preferable.

2. Prepare a reply to the letter on the page opposite. Use the notes given on page 184 to help you.

HALLWIN & EDGAR
421 OXFORD STREET LONDON W1R 1RF

Technical Supplies Ltd
Bermondsey   13th May 19..

Dear Sirs

We were very surprised when, after our talk with your clerk yesterday, the goods which he had promised would be sent off immediately did not arrive this morning. This is by no means the first time that we have had to complain about delay on your part in fulfilling our orders. Less than six months ago we made a similar complaint. Although we know that the materials you supply are as good as you claim, punctual delivery is as important to us as quality, since we cannot retain our customers unless we can fulfil all their orders without delay.

There is one other matter to which we should like to draw your attention. Three days ago we received the enclosed bill, in which we are charged for materials that have not been supplied. We shall be glad to have your explanation.

We hope that both these matters will receive prompt attention and that we shall not have to take our business to any other firm for, as you know, we have a high opinion of your materials.

Yours faithfully
Hallwin & Edgar

Encl.

Notes for Reply (a) Goods were dispatched by carrier immediately and should have arrived by now. A hold-up at carrier's depot.

(b) Materials charged on returned bill were sent. A receipt signed by warehouseman is held by Technical Supplies Ltd.

3. Blane & Co, Lancaster (Telegraphic address BLANECO, Lancaster) send a telegram to McConnell & Co, Belfast (Telegraphic address LINEN, Belfast) asking them to increase their Order No. 363 to 24 dozen men's handkerchiefs. Delivery urgent.

    Write out this telegram; it must not exceed 12 words. Also, write the reply.

4. Parke, James & Co, Harper Street, Newcastle upon Tyne NE3 5QH send the following order to Midland Tools Ltd, Coventry CV3 8EB—

    1 Lathe—surfacing, sliding and screw-cutting
        as shown on p 10 of catalogue No 6

    to be sent by goods train, carriage forward to their address. Delivery within one month.

    Write the order letter, also the letter acknowledging order.

5. Make a précis, not more than 120 words, of the correspondence that appears on the following three pages. Show also the list you made before writing the précis of the most important points in each letter.

1.

Mr Thomas Johnson, Chartered Accountant, 8 Pool Road, Blackpool FY3 7SG, To Messrs Wilson & Sons, Merchants, 34 Liver House, Liverpool L69 4AN.

8 February 19..

With reference to my letter of 25 January I have been informed that your customers Messrs Jameson & Co have announced their insolvency.

Nothing is known at the moment about their assets and liabilities, although I have reason to believe that the position is not very favourable. As soon as I have definite and reliable information I shall write to you again.

If you wish me to represent you in this matter I shall be obliged if you will send me a statement of your account and instructions to act on your behalf.

2.

Messrs Wilson & Sons to Mr Thos Johnson

10 February 19..

We are surprised to learn from your letter of 8 February that Messrs Jameson & Co have declared their insolvency. Our interest in their business amounts, unfortunately, to £550.

We enclose a statement of our account, and we shall be glad if you will kindly act for us in this matter.

3.

Mr Thos Johnson to Messrs Wilson & Sons

4 March 19..

I have received your letter of 10 February enclosing a statement of your account with Messrs Jameson & Co and authorising me to act on your behalf.

At a meeting of the creditors held on 2 March it was agreed to accept a composition of 70p in the £. It was fully explained at the meeting that if the estate were declared bankrupt, no more than 52½p in the £ would be realised, and that no fault could be attached to Messrs Jameson & Co.

Although the amount of your loss is large, I think that in the circumstances you will agree that the best course has been taken.

Payment will be made in three dividends of equal amounts, on 1 July, 1 September and 1 November of this year, and the three solvent guarantors are security for the carrying out of the arrangements.

If you wish, I shall be pleased to collect your dividends as they become due, and to hold them awaiting your instructions.

Messrs Wilson & Sons To Mr Thos Johnson

7 March 19..

We have received your letter of 4 March informing us that Messrs Jameson & Co have made a composition of 70p in the £. We agree to this arrangement.

As suggested, we shall be obliged if you will collect our dividends when due and hold them pending further instructions from us.

TEST No 4

1. For each of the following words supply one synonym and one antonym—

    concise, prevalent, oblivious, doubtful, clarity, perpendicular, reluctant.

2. (*a*) Add prefixes to form the negatives of the following words—

    legible, responsible, logical, favour, trust, relevant, trustworthy, possible, eligible, sensible.

   (*b*) Add suffixes to the following to form new words—

    friend, defer, futile, refer, state, treat.

3. A wholesaler has received a special consignment of goods. He offers them to a retailer at reduced prices.

    Write this letter and also the reply.

4. The telephone bell rings and you answer it. An important client is calling, asking to speak to your employer who is out, but who will be back within half-an-hour.

    Give a complete account of this telephone conversation; your answer must be given in direct speech.

5. Write a letter, as from yourself, to Messrs Anderson & Bell, House Agents, 50 Kingston Road, Reading RG2 9ET asking whether they have on their books a semi-detached

house with three bedrooms and two reception rooms etc, or a five roomed bungalow. Price not to exceed £9,750. Garage essential and a small garden desirable. In residential area, with shopping centre within easy reach.

6. On 27th May West Sugar Refineries Ltd, Greenock send a letter to Stagg & Co, Esplanade North, Dundee DD7 7JU enclosing statement of account for sugar supplied on 9th May. They state that $2\frac{1}{2}\%$ discount will be allowed if the account is paid within thirty days.

On 27th June West Sugar Refineries Ltd end reminder about outstanding account to Stagg & Co and ask for payment. They also state that no discount can now be allowed.

On 15th July West Sugar Refineries Ltd send a second reminder about account to Stagg & Co. They ask for payment by return.

On 27th July West Sugar Refineries Ltd send a final reminder to Stagg & Co and threaten legal proceedings if the account is not paid within seven days.

Write these four letters.

TEST No 5

1. Study the following examples of business jargon and re-write each one in simple and direct language—
   (a) Your esteemed favour to hand
   (b) We beg to acknowledge receipt of your communication
   (c) We thank you for same
   (d) We beg to assure you
   (e) We enclose herewith
   (f) It is felt to be necessary
   (g) We shall take a very early opportunity of writing
   (h) It has been brought to our notice

2. Add the correct prepositions to the following—
   agree, deficient, inspired, intrude, ineligible, correspond, prevail, responsible, wait, call, part, disappointed.

3. Give the meaning of—
   pro tem, PS, E & OE, ad lib, IOM, stet, 8vo, fcp. pro forma.

4. As secretary, write a short report (about 200 words) on—
   The activities of your Tennis Club during the past year.

5. Write the minutes of a Board of Directors' meeting, giving the name of firm, date and time. Include the following—
   (*a*) minutes of last meeting to be confirmed
   (*b*) presentation of financial statement
   and three other items.

6. On 2nd May Dennis Jackson & Co, Commerce Road, Swansea SA3 5BD complain to Cubana & Co, Oxford Street, London WIR 1RF that the cigars supplied to them on 24th April were not according to order. Strong flavoured cigars were sent instead of mild cigars. They ask for an explanation and immediate replacement. The cigars supplied are being returned.

   Write a letter of complaint.

   Cubana & Co express regret for the mistake and state they are sending the mild cigars at once.

   Write their reply.

TEST No 6

1. Rewrite each of the following sentences correctly.
   (*a*) I had hoped to have found that more progress had been made.
   (*b*) To all appearances he seems incapable of carrying out the work.
   (*c*) The one is equally as bad as the other.
   (*d*) I dislike him interrupting me so rudely.
   (*e*) If one has to finally decide whether to spend a holiday at home or abroad, the state of their finances will determine it.
   (*f*) This lift must only be used by the staff.

2. Use the following words in sentences to show their meanings—
   urban   treatise   ordinance   hoard
   urbane   treaties   ordnance   horde

3. Write your letter of application to the following advertisement—

Shorthand-typist required by Shipping Company. Good qualifications in English, shorthand, typewriting essential. Knowledge of book-keeping an advantage. 5-day week. Staff canteen. Excellent prospects. Apply to Personnel Officer, Sanderson Shipping Co, Hope Street, Glasgow C2 giving full particulars of age, experience, reference, etc.

4. Danks & Co, 111 New Bond Street, London W1Y 9AB are sending their junior partner, Mr Geoffrey Danks to Munich to attend the World Trade Fair in order to meet prospective buyers of their goods. They send a letter of introduction to Herren Lange & Co, Munich.

    Write the letter of introduction giving the necessary details.

5. Write a summary of the following passage; your précis should not exceed 130 words.

Saigon—Istanbul Railway

The Japanese Transport Ministry is preparing to make a detailed study of a proposal to build a railway across Southern Asia, from Saigon to Istanbul.

The proposal emanates from Japanese business and official circles interested in the promotion of major construction projects overseas, possible under the protection of the Asian Development Bank.

The inaugural meeting of the ADB will take place in Tokyo on November 24–26, and Japan is expected to play the leading role in the organization.

The rather ambitious Transport Ministry plan was first published in yesterday's edition of the *Nihon Keizai*, a leading Japanese economic daily. According to the newspaper the railway would link Pnom Penh, Bangkok, Rangoon, Calcutta, New Delhi, Rawalpindi, Karachi, Baghdad and Ankara. A very tentative estimate of over £3,000m has been given for the construction costs.

These are still very early days. The Transport Ministry will not launch its basic survey of the plan until the next fiscal year–that is, from April 19.... The plan itself has not been formally proposed to the United Regional body, the

Economic Commission for Asia and the Far East (ECAFE), although such a proposal may be made, as ECAFE could play an important co-ordinating role.

Meanwhile the Construction Ministry has commenced studies for a purely Japanese project—construction of a six to ten mile long tunnel under Tokyo Bay. There are also proposals for a causeway or bridge across the bay, at a possible cost of £200m. Communications between outlying parts of the Tokyo Metropolis have become increasingly difficult.

A more prosaic and much more realistic proposal for Asian co-operation, is likely to be made by Japan at a forthcoming conference on agricultural developments in South East Asia, scheduled to be held in Tokyo on December 6, 19 . . . . This is for the establishment of an agricultural development fund. The fund might function as an organ within the Asian Development Bank.

The agricultural conference will follow up a South-East Asian ministerial conference on economic development held in Tokyo last April—the first major international meeting proposed by Japan since the war.

TEST No 7

1. Write a report of about 250 words on a search for suitable accommodation for a new manager and his family.

2. The Typewriter Supply Co Ltd have had the contract for the maintenance of all the office machines of your firm. Lately the quality of work has deteriorated.

   Write a suitable letter of complaint.

3. You are secretary to an Overseas Students Club and have been asked by the committee to write a letter of thanks to the retiring Club President.

   Write this letter and invite him to a Presentation Dinner; inform him that he will be required to reply to the toast of "Club Presidents."

4. The switchboard operator has referred a call to your extension by mistake. The caller wishes to speak to Mr Hobson of the Export Department.

192 ENGLISH FOR BUSINESS

Write down, in direct speech, both sides of the conversation with this caller, in which you explain the mistake and ask the operator to transfer the call.

5. A customer has written complaining of incivility on the part of a member of the sales staff of your firm. This customer is well-known for his overbearing manner.

Write a tactful letter to him.

6. The managers of the Branches are coming to Head Office for a conference. They are to stay for three days at the same hotel; a room will be required for conference purposes during the time of their visit.

Write a letter of inquiry to the hotel giving full details of the requirements.

TEST No 8

1. Write a short essay of about 350 words on Television Advertising.

2. You have been sent by the Managing Director of your firm to make preliminary inquiries regarding a possible site for a factory in north-east Scotland.

Write the report, supplying names.

3. Write a letter complaining about the quality of school blazers supplied by a manufacturer. The blazers have faded after only a short period of wear.

Write also the reply from the manufacturer.

4. What are the characteristics of a good précis? What points should be observed in writing a précis of the correspondence involved in a business transaction?

5. Write an explanatory paragraph about the use of "Messrs." When would you—
   (a) use this form of address?
   (b) not use it?

Give two examples of (a) and (b).

6. What, in your view, are the essential differences between a secretary and a shorthand-typist? Write your answer in four paragraphs, not exceeding 250 words.